New Jersey's Great Gardens

Rudolph W. Van der Goot Rose Garden at Colonial Park

New Jersey's Great Gardens

A Four-Season Guide
to 125 Public Gardens,
Parks, and Arboretums

Arline Zatz

*Photographs by Arline Zatz
and Joel L. Zatz*

The Countryman Press
Woodstock, Vermont

Copyright © 1999 by Arline Zatz
First Edition

Library of Congress Cataloging-in-Publication Data
Zatz, Arline
New Jersey's Great Gardens : a four-season guide to 125 public gardens, parks, and arboretums / Arline Zatz
p.   cm.
Includes index.
ISBN 0-88150-356-8
1. Gardens—New Jersey—Guidebooks. 2. Arboretums—New Jersey—Guidebooks. 3. New Jersey—Guidebooks. I. Title.
SB466.U65N549 1999
712'.025'749—DC 21   98-13750

Published by The Countryman Press, PO Box 748, Woodstock, Vermont 05091
Distributed by W.W. Norton and Company, 500 Fifth Avenue, New York, New York 10110

Cover and text design by Sally Sherman
Cover photographs by Joel L. Zatz
Maps by Harry Wirtz, © 1999 The Countryman Press

Printed in Canada
10 9 8 7 6 5 4 3 2

Dedication

Though nothing can bring back the hour
Of splendour in the grass, of glory in the flower,
We will grieve not, rather find
Strength in what remains behind.

—WILLIAM WORDSWORTH

This book is in memory of two dear friends, Dr. Florence Segelman and Ferris Meigs Stout, who shared a love for gardening and all living creatures.

As a pharmacognocist, Flo's plant research enlightened the world, but her bed of hostas was her secret pleasure and treasure. When she shared a few of the plants with me, I was honored, and as they awaken each spring, I am filled with joy.

Ferris, a bighearted bear of a man, was a crackerjack chemical engineer and patent agent. While he was a whiz at solving problems for his clients, it was his friends who chuckled as he told jokes in a way no one else on earth could, and who appreciated his good nature.

Both of these individuals disappeared from my life all too soon, but I am thankful to them for enriching it and for the wonderful memories I will cherish forever. Above all, I shall remember our friendship. You are both truly missed.

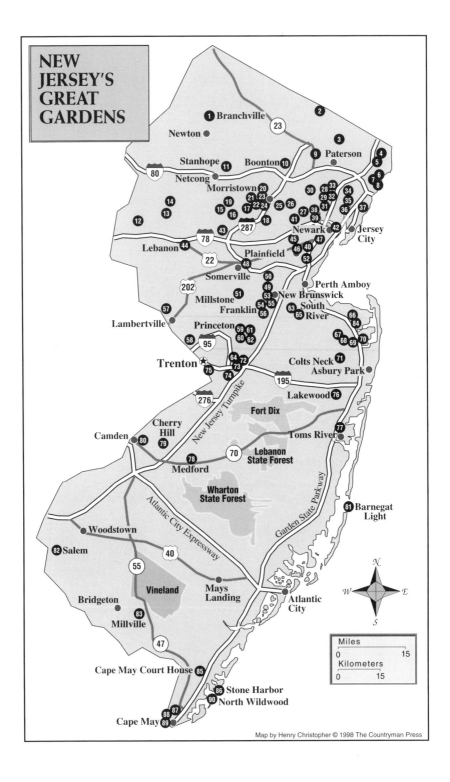

NEW JERSEY'S GREAT GARDENS

1 Branchville
Newton ●
Stanhope   Boonton 10
Netcong   9 Paterson
Morristown   30   28 33   34
20   29 32   35
21 23   31 38   36
22 24   27 38   37
15 19   25 26   39
16   18   41   42   Jersey
43   287   Newark   City
Lebanon 44   45   47
22   46 40
Plainfield   52
48
Somerville   50
202   49   53   Perth Amboy
Millstone 51   New Brunswick
Franklin   54 55   63 South
56   65 River   66 84
Lambertville   57   67 70
Princeton   59 61   68 69
58   60 62
95   64 72   Colts Neck 71
Trenton ★   73   Asbury Park
75   74
276   195
Lakewood 76
Fort Dix
Cherry   77
Camden   Hill   Toms River
80   79   Lebanon
78   70   State Forest
Medford
Wharton
State Forest
81 Barnegat
Light
Woodstown
82 Salem
40
55
Vineland   Mays
Bridgeton   Landing
83   Atlantic
Millville   City
47
Cape May Court House 85
86 Stone Harbor
90 North Wildwood
Cape May 88 87
89

N
W   E
S

Miles
0 ————— 15
Kilometers
0 ————— 15

Map by Henry Christopher © 1998 The Countryman Press

Contents

III. SOUTHERN NEW JERSEY

Acknowledgments

I owe thanks to my publisher, The Countryman Press, for listening to my idea for this book and putting it into print; to editor in chief Helen Whybrow, for her valued opinions and constructive input; and to managing editor Ann Kraybill, who asked interesting questions, fine-tuned my words, and had infinite patience.

I am also grateful to the many organizations, garden directors, park superintendents, and other individuals who helped me gather the necessary information for each garden; the countless volunteers who donate their time and effort to the gardens and took time out from their busy schedules to return my phone calls; and the tour guides who filled me in on important facts.

Along the way, a few of the names of those who helped disappeared into my heaps of notes, but to all of you I offer my sincere thanks. I offer thanks as well to: Jack Aprill, Leaming's Run Gardens & Colonial Farm; Alan Archer, Deep Cut Park; Allison Barnett, Van Vleck Gardens; John Benton, New Jersey Forest Resource Education Center; Allene Berian, Allen House; Bob Butell, Tenafly Parks; Mary Cherington, Cannonball House; Phyllis Coldebella, Nutley Parks Department; Jim Consolloy, Prospect Gardens; Madeline Dennis, Flat Rock Brook; Steve Dickinson, Bobbink Memorial Garden; Hazel England, Lord Stirling Park; Scott Fenbart, Van Saun Park; Jonathan Forsell, Cook College; Mary Jane Frankel, The Manor; Denise Fuchs, Phoenix House; Marion Glaspey, The Wetlands Institute Gardens; Lee Ellen Griffith, Monmouth County Historical Association; Jennifer L. Kaplan, Delaware-Raritan Girl Scout Council; Ingrid Leonard, Kingsland Manor; Beverly Lichtenstein, Garden Club of New Jersey; Diane Lingsch, Allaire State Park; Gladys Lockyer, Waterloo Village; Rev. Beatus T. Lucey, Delbarton School;

Ronnie Mahoney, Ocean County College Arboretum; Newt Meeker, Maplewood Superintendent of Parks; Denise Mikics, *New Jersey Outdoors* magazine; John Mills, Princeton Battlefield State Park; Steve Murray, Superintendent of North Wildwood Parks; Krista Murphy, The James Rose Center; Ruth Nicoll, The Hermitage; Tom Nolan, St. Mary's Roman Catholic Church Butterfly Garden; Rose Pepe, Georgian Court College; Janet Peterson, Wheaton Village; Dafnia Pontius, Drumthwacket; Peter Punzi, McFaul Environmental Center; Kathy Rafferty, Crane Museum Gardens; Harry Robinson, Township of Hamilton Grounds Supervisor; Sean Ryan, County of Union Parks and Recreation; Sally Sachs, Circle Gardens; Marie Savoia, R.F.D. Garden Club; Jane Stein, Alice Ransom Dreyfuss Memorial Garden; Paul Tarlowe, Pequest Education Center; Dean S. Thomas, Thomas Publications; Sister Agnes Vincent, Shakespeare Garden at College of St. Elizabeth; Dr. Sara Webb, Drew University/Zuck Arboretum; Julie Wilson, The Garden Club of Montclair, Inc.; Ruth Yablonsky, Watchung Reservation; Charlie Zafonte, Morris County Parks System; and Denise Dale Zemlansky, Kuser Farm Mansion.

Friends, including Jean Bayrock, Dawn Clements, Veronika Diener, Virginia Edwards, Lila Garfield, Laura and Marvin Mausner, Denise Mikics, Janet Savin, and Mary Ann Simon, played an important role, too, especially when they forgave me for not socializing on days when I had to scout gardens, or when I was deep in thought working on my computer. As was the case with my previous books, I never tired of hearing my dear friend, Mary Elwood, relay cheery wishes that helped to make my words flow.

Hearty thanks, too, to my son, Dr. David Zatz, for his great suggestions; to his wife, Dr. Kate Zatz, for challenging me to find and describe each of New Jersey's great gardens; to Dr. Ellen Hulme, for her words of wisdom; and to Dr. Felicia Oliver-Smith, who, many years ago, encouraged me to write my first book.

Last, special thanks, big hugs, and lots of love to my husband, Joel, for his role in writing directions to each garden so I wouldn't get lost, for his photographic skills, and most of all, for the pleasure of his company on many of the glorious garden outings.

Introduction

> *If the day and the night are such that you greet them with joy, and life emits a fragrance like flowers and sweet-scented herbs . . . that is your success.*
>
> —HENRY DAVID THOREAU

People often wonder why New Jersey was nicknamed the Garden State. Theories abound, but no one knows for sure. Perhaps it's because we're blessed with so many gardens, or because of the truck farms that were so popular at the turn of the last century. Some people are of the opinion that the nickname was adopted in 1876 when the Honorable Abraham Browning gave an address on New Jersey at the Centennial Exhibition in Philadelphia, comparing this state to an immense barrel that was filled with good things to eat and open at both ends. He painted a picture of Pennsylvania grabbing its contents from one side and New Yorkers grabbing from the other, and referred to New Jersey as the "Garden State." Whatever the reason for the nickname, New Jersey's gardens have been essential for providing shelter, food, medicinals, privacy, and beauty, and for educating us on the wonders of plant life.

The 125 gardens described in this guide are located throughout the Garden State. The tulips in Warinanco Park Gardens put on a glorious show each spring; the Marquand Park arboretum features 200 species of trees; at Grounds for Sculpture, dozens of three-dimensional works of art grace a lush, gently rolling lawn amid shrubs and trees; and at Pavilion Circle Gardens, local residents have willingly and joyfully joined together to create an incredible display of individual garden areas filled with an abundance of flowers, shrubs, and places to sit. You'll find gardens ranging from hundreds of acres to pocket-sized gems; rock gardens sporting tiny plants tucked between the cracks; knot gardens in interesting shapes; herb gardens that are a sensory delight; kitchen gardens of yesteryear; scent gardens emitting fragrant aromas; memorial gardens in tribute to individuals; and even a delightful garden for the vision-impaired. The many arboretums of New Jersey are wonderful places to seek out on hot, sunny days, for the natural canopy of leaves lowers temperatures and provides shade. Here you'll often find the red oak—officially selected as the state tree in 1950 for its strength, dignity, structural beauty, and long life. Finally, many of the gardens described here are adjacent to historic sites and mansions where guided tours are offered.

Gardens are usually defined as places where flowers or other plants are grown. After visiting New Jersey's gardens, arboretums, and woods, I feel this definition is incomplete: A garden is also a haven where one can escape from everyday stress, enjoy peace and quiet, and awaken the senses. In visiting these gardens, I was charmed by the plantings, renewed by watching the wildlife, and relaxed while inhaling the fragrance of the flowers. I hope you will be, too. Have a great horticultural adventure in this glorious Garden State!

SPECIFICS

The pages ahead provide detailed information on 125 great gardens to visit within the Garden State. Each chapter describes highlighted plantings, location, admission, hours, facilities, and events, and identifies peak season when relevant. While most gardens do not charge admission, it's always best to call before starting out, especially because hours and other policies may change.

TIPS FOR VISITING THESE GARDENS:

- ❧ Use a waterproof sunscreen, with an SPF of 15 or more, generously.
- ❧ Use insect repellent and avoid perfume, since it attracts insects.
- ❧ Don a hat, dress in comfortable clothing and shoes, and wear sunglasses.
- ❧ Take plenty of water.
- ❧ Bring flower, fern, tree, or bird identification books; a pad and pen for taking notes; a magnifying glass; binoculars if you're a birdwatcher; and a camera with lots of film.
- ❧ Schedule visits during early morning or late afternoon, and always call before starting out; hours are subject to change.
- ❧ Please do not pick flowers or remove plants from any garden.
- ❧ Stay on designated paths.
- ❧ Leave pets at home and supervise children.
- ❧ Be cautious about coming into contact with plants because certain species can cause severe skin irritation, blisters, and itching. Learn to recognize poison ivy: Remember, leaves of three, let it be.

Northern
New Jersey

1

Tillman Ravine Woods

LOCATION ❧ Sussex County
Stokes State Forest
Struble Road off Route 206
Branchville 07826
973-948-3820

GARDEN SIZE ❧ 375 acres

ADMISSION ❧ No charge

WHEN TO VISIT ❧ Dawn to dusk daily, year-round. The road is closed during winter months.

HIGHLIGHTS ❧ Lush woods, wildflowers in spring, and geological formations

FACILITIES ❧ Outhouse

Tillman Ravine Woods is the perfect place to experience a spiritual awakening, for here, beneath towering hemlocks, with melodious sounds of the flowing stream and tiny waterfalls, there is a sense of total serenity.

You don't have to walk far from the parking area to enjoy the surroundings: As soon as you enter the woods, the scenery is spectacular. However, the self-guiding, circular, mile-long trail is quite interesting. Picnic next to the stream, listen to the bird calls, or to the branches whispering as they touch in the slightest breeze. If you've braved the park in winter and walk along the closed road, you'll find the frozen milky-white stream in brilliant contrast to the deep emerald glow of the evergreens.

At the beginning of the trail, there's a stand of red and yellow pines that were planted more than 50 years ago as part of a Civilian Conservation Corps project. How do you tell them apart? While both produce needles in clusters of two, the yellow (short-leaf) pine has 3- to 5-inch needles and a prickly cone, while the red pine has smoothly edged cones and 6-inch needles.

In a short distance, the hemlocks appear, graceful evergreens shaped like pyramids with needles about a half inch long that spread out on either side of the branches. Turn over the flat needles to see the two distinctive silver stripes on the underside for a positive identification. This beauty also has tiny cones hanging on the tips of its branches year-round. Hemlocks can live more than 150 years and may reach 112 feet. While these have thrived in this area for years because of the acid soil and humid air, they may not last much longer due to a woolly adelgid infestation that has threatened their health since the early 1990s.

The Upper Falls, encountered after crossing a small wooden bridge, is a great place to pause, for here you can see and hear the bubbling water as you scan the area. Tillman Ravine, a relatively young geologic feature, developed when the last glacier started to melt about 10,000 years ago and small streams began to flow from springs farther up on the ridge. The energy of the water flowing downhill eroded the rock; in time, this new, deep valley will erode into a broad, gentle valley that is characteristic of a mature stream.

June and early July are a great time to visit, when huge stands of rhododendron burst into color. Trillium, with a whorl of three leaves at its top, blooms in late June; you'll also find fallen hemlocks that are covered with varnish conk, an unusual fungus that looks as though it was sprayed with a coat of lacquer. Partridgeberry, a trailing plant with scarlet berries, is in bloom from July through November; and jack-in-the-pulpit, with its purple hood arched over a stalk, is scattered throughout the forest floor.

The ridge trail appears again at the next bridge and continues beneath stately oak and maple. In addition to the numerous hemlocks, there's also a mixture of black birch, black cherry, flowering dogwood, hickory, sycamore, and tulip trees.

NOTE: While sneakers are fine for these woods, a sturdy walking shoe will prevent your toes from being stubbed on the boulders.

2

Skylands, the New Jersey State Botanical Garden

LOCATION ❧ Passaic County
Ringwood State Park
Morris Road off Sloatsburg Road
Ringwood 07456
973-962-9534
web site: www.njskylandsgarden.org

GARDEN SIZE ❧ More than 96 acres of formal gardens; hundreds of acres of woodlands and meadows

ADMISSION ❧ *Gardens:* No charge except for parking fee weekends during summer months. *House:* Fee.

WHEN TO VISIT ❧ *Gardens:* Open 8 AM–8 PM daily, year-round. *House:* Open only on certain dates; call for a schedule.

HIGHLIGHTS ❧ Formal and informal gardens with unusual plant species from around the world; fantastic vistas; historic manor house

FACILITIES ❧ Rest room; limited wheelchair access. Pets and picnicking are not allowed.

EVENTS ❧ Annual plant sale; educational programs such as talks on how to raise ferns, garden design, and horticulture in foreign countries, sponsored by the Skylands Association. Call for a schedule.

Skylands, the New Jersey State Botanical Garden, is a unique country estate featuring elegantly landscaped grounds, historic buildings, and a vast collection of unusual plant species from around the world.

Here in the Ramapo Mountains overlooking the Wanaque Reservoir, surrounded by 5,000 acres within Ringwood State Park, sits Skylands. Hundreds of trees and lovely themed gardens, many dating to 1891, are set on vast, gently rolling lawns affording unbelievable vistas. Also on the property are a carriage house, now used as a visitor center; several greenhouses; landscaped terraces; and a 44-room Tudor mansion.

Wear comfortable shoes when you visit Skylands; there's lots of walking between the various garden areas. There are also lots of places to rest, however, while you enjoy the scenery. If you want to admire the pink blossoms along the half-mile Crab Apple Vista, come in mid-May. More than 150 of these beauties stand in a row, marking the boundary between the formal gardens surrounding the manor and the informal and wildflower gardens at the foot of the Ramapos. At the Vista's south end is a horse chestnut collection; to the east is Swan Pond Meadow, a water meadow home to moisture-loving plants, including the rare fringed gentian and many varieties of willow.

The formal Annual Garden, with plantings that vary from year to year and bloom from June to the first frost, follows the original layout, while the Perennial Border Garden, at its peak in April, June, and September, is slowly being restored to the original plan designed by Clarence McKenzie Lewis, one of its owners. May through June is the best time to visit the Lilac Garden on the East Lawn. This collection contains many varieties of eight species of lilac, including one of the first that Lewis acquired in 1923, the Persian lilac. In 1928, the Japanese tree lilac and the Chinese lilac were purchased, along with French hybrids. Lilacs, with their wonderful aroma and showy blooms, have been popular since colonial times. A dwarf horse chestnut and a rare *Adina rubella* shrub are also in this section.

In June, sweet bay magnolias perfume the Magnolia Walk. These southern trees must be wrapped each winter to protect them from the cold; Lewis planted them close to the house both to shelter them and so that he could enjoy their fragrance through the open windows. Scented viburnum and honeysuckle fill the understory beneath the magnolias; east of the walk you'll find an unusual columnar form of the sugar maple. To the west, you'll find a Kentucky coffee tree sporting interesting bark and thick branches, especially noticeable in winter. A Japanese pagoda tree and a golden-rain tree, which both bloom in August, stand nearby.

On a hot summer's day, the stone bench in the Peony Garden is handy, situated as it is beneath a canopy of American hemlocks. Nearby are shrubby, woody-stemmed tree peonies native to western China, and background shrub plants, including weigela, buddleia, beauty bush, and deutzia, that were popular during the Victorian era.

Surrounding the reflecting pool are huge plantings of azalea and

An eagle adorns the entrance to Skylands.

rhododendron, particularly eye-catching during mid-May to June, when they bloom in a variety of colors. Cultivars include the white 'Boule de Neige', 'Pink Twins', and the vivid red 'Nova Zembla'. The Japanese maple at the head of the pool and the sourwood are striking in autumn, as is the mature mountain silver-bell tree. The Winter Garden, planted between 1927 and 1928, consists of an evergreen collection of varying shades and textures, while on the west side stands New Jersey's largest Jeffrey pine. To the east, a weeping beech is adjacent to a century-old upright beech and a Japanese umbrella pine planted between 1891 and 1920. An Algerian fir grown from seed in 1931 bears 7-inch purple cones, and an Atlas cedar purchased by Lewis in 1928 can also be seen in this area.

Skylands forms the heart of a property that Francis Lynde Stetson (1846–1920) assembled from pioneer farmsteads in the surrounding area. Naming his country estate Skylands Farms, he built a Queen Anne Victorian mansion of native granite and created a working farm with more than 30 outbuildings, gardens, and a vast lawn he used as a nine-hole golf course. He chose Samuel Parsons Jr., a protégé of Frederick Law Olmsted, to lay out his estate. Here, the prominent New York lawyer entertained friends that included Grover Cleveland, Andrew Carnegie, Ethel Barrymore, and J.P. Morgan. In 1922 the property was sold to Clarence McKenzie Lewis (1877–1959), an investment banker and trustee of the New York Botanical Garden. Lewis turned Skylands into a horticultural showplace, tore down the original house, and on the site built the existing Jacobean mansion, of native granite like the original, intentionally making it appear centuries old by incorporating a weathered stone facade and sags and ripples in the slate roof. The firm of Vitale and Geiffert designed the gardens, and most of the trees around the house, including the magnificent copper beeches, were planted at that time.

Designated as New Jersey's official Botanical Garden in 1984 by Governor Thomas Kean, and listed on the State and National Registers of Historic Places in 1990, this is the place to find something in bloom throughout the year, including January, when the southern wall of the manor house is covered with the bright yellow flowers of the clinging winter jasmine. Many of the plantings seen here today were brought in by Clarence McKenzie Lewis, who was also a renowned amateur horticulturist. Lewis spent three decades exchanging plants and information with nurserymen, arboretums, and botanical gardens worldwide, while collecting plants he thought would grow at Skylands from such diverse habitat as New Jersey's Pine Barrens, Afghanistan, and the Belgian Congo (now Zaire).

The Skylands Association was founded in 1976 to assist the state garden staff in the preservation and restoration of Skylands and its historic Manor House, and to develop educational programs for the public. Thanks are due to the dozens of volunteer members, both amateur and trained horticulturists, who help keep the garden beautiful.

NOTE: There are miles of hiking trails within the park at Skylands. In season, don a bathing suit and enjoy a cool dip in nearby Shepherd Lake, or rent a canoe or paddleboat. Take a picnic lunch; restaurants are a distance away.

3

McFaul Gardens

LOCATION ❧ Bergen County
James A. McFaul Environmental Center
Crescent Avenue (north of Route 208)
Wyckoff 07481
201-891-5571

GARDEN SIZE ❧ More than 80 acres

ADMISSION ❧ No charge

WHEN TO VISIT ❧ Daily 8:30 AM–7:30 PM, year-round, except
Christmas and New Year's Day

HIGHLIGHTS ❧ A huge variety of gardens and plantings

FACILITIES ❧ Rest room, water, benches; partially handicapped-
accessible garden areas, handicapped-accessible
boardwalk with observation deck; picnic tables;
nature library

EVENTS ❧ Talks, slide shows, films, and walks Saturday,
Sunday, and Tuesday at 2 PM.

The James A. McFaul Environmental Center, dedicated to the horticultural sciences, has been fulfilling its goal to educate people in becoming aware of their natural surroundings and interacting with flora and
fauna, through both active and passive programming, since 1968.
Plantings began with thousands of daffodils, hyacinths, tulips, and a
variety of shrubs donated by individuals and the Bergen County
Federation of Garden Clubs.

Today, thanks to a full-time horticulturist, a landscape supervisor,
dedicated volunteers from the Bergen County Master Gardener's
Program, and interns from Bergen Community College, the grounds are
filled with a bounty of magnificent flowers, shrubs, and native and ornamental trees.

In the Wildflower Fields, English aster, six species of goldenrod,

One of the many lovely areas at McFaul Gardens

brown-eyed Susan, cosmos, boneset, thistle, Indian blanket, and other beauties spread as they wish. Nearby, the Herb Garden, begun approximately 20 years ago beneath the shade of a tall Austrian pine, boasts two semicircular areas planted with an array of Egyptian chives, savory, lovage, borage, parsley, oregano, lavender, tansy, sage, bronze fennel, and soapwort.

The Dwarf Conifer Garden began with seed a Master Gardener supplied. In the Secret Scented Garden, clematis climbs up a trellis, roses are surrounded by stands of bamboo, and plantings include lemon and silver thyme and oregano. At the Water Garden, you may catch sight of a muskrat nibbling a water lily, see a few fish hunting for a tasty morsel near the surface of the pond, or spot one of the great blue herons and egrets that often flock to this area.

Beneath a lovely weeping willow you'll find the Herbal Seat, planted with thyme to provide a soft and aromatic cushion. Seats like this were fashionable in English gardens in the 1500s. The Natural Succession Field is a vast grassy area that's mowed one section at a time so visitors can note its various stages of growth. Take a short stroll up the nearby hill; it leads through a woody area where trees are marked with memorial plaques. There are also lots of shrubs in this area, including the autumn olive, which former horticulturist Peter Punzi described as "a fast grower from China that's the first to colonize an area." The vast variety of trees includes black cherry, star magnolia, beech, Colorado spruce, holly, hawthorn, devil's-walking-stick, fir, hemlock, and umbrella pine.

Don't miss the Azalea and Rhododendron Garden, delightful during spring; or the newly planted Rose Garden, filled with miniature and old-fashioned roses; or the Hummingbird and Butterfly Garden, stocked with cardinal flower, butterfly weed, milkweed, and other plants designed to attract a crowd. Returning to your car, exit a road lined with hornbeams.

NOTE: The McFaul Environmental Center, a member of the Association of Zoological Horticulture and the American Association of Botanical Gardens and Arboreta, publishes *The Horticultural Harbinger*, a quarterly newsletter promoting horticultural education and activities. As a bonus, explore the center's exhibit hall. It's filled with live native animals, aquariums, and natural history displays, and overlooks a pond popular with wildlife.

4

United Water Xeriscape Garden

LOCATION ❧ Bergen County
Haworth Water Treatment Plant
200 Lakeshore Drive
Haworth 07640
201-767-9300

GARDEN SIZE ❧ Less than ½ acre

ADMISSION ❧ No charge

WHEN TO VISIT ❧ Dawn to dusk daily, year-round

HIGHLIGHTS ❧ Demonstration Xeriscape garden with perennial, tree, shrub, flower, and ground cover plantings, bird-watching

FACILITIES ❧ Benches

Xeriscape, from the Greek word *xero*, meaning "dry," refers to an environment in which plants can thrive with very little rainfall. In 1995, the United Water Company unveiled a Xeriscape garden on the grounds of the Haworth Water Treatment Plant with the hope that, in seeing this jewel of a garden, visitors would be encouraged to plan similiar low-maintenance gardens on their properties. Xeriscape gardens can save counties millions of gallons of water; at the same time, through Xeriscape gardening individuals can eliminate the tiresome chore of dragging out a hose each day. If you're interested in starting a garden of this type, this is the perfect place to learn the ropes. Bring a pad and pencil to take notes; each species is labeled.

With the help of DeRosa Landscaping of Montvale and the Rutgers Cooperative Extension Service in Bergen County, a rich mixture of perennial grasses, flowers, shrubs, and trees purchased from local nurseries were planted here. Not only have they survived, but they are thriving. Tucked

The United Water Xeriscape Garden educates the public about water conservation.

in among the rocks are hens-and-chicks, a spreading succulent with thick leaves in rosettes, and stonecrop sedum, a tiny, elegant specimen that grows year-round. Its reddish-green leaf buds appear in early spring, followed by 2-foot-tall shoots with succulent foliage. By late August, tiny clusters of pink flowers are in bloom. During late fall the blossoms dry out, but they remain on the plant and are attractive through winter.

The attractive ground covers include sweet woodruff, smelling like new-mown hay and sporting tiny white flowers from May to June; creeping phlox, producing white flowers during April and May; forever green thyme; and mat-forming bearberry, with shiny, evergreen leaves and pendulous white to pink flowers.

The pincushion flower—often referred to as butterfly blue for its blue flower whose center resembles a pincushion—is dazzling, as is black-eyed Susan with its daisylike flower, and the Lenten rose, with its cup-shaped blooms that appear in early spring.

Hostas with glossy green heart-shaped leaves decorated with gleaming white margins light up the shady areas. The tall, lustrous fronds of the ostrich fern can be viewed in the moist section of the garden, which is maintained with the liberal use of mulch and water-conserving soak hoses. Other beauties include Solomon's seal, Old English lavender, bleeding heart, candytuft, and a variety of grasses including sheep fescue and variegated Japanese sedge.

Don't hesitate to visit on a sunny, hot day because the tall pines form a thick, cool canopy. And the garden continues to flower throughout the summer: During July and August, daylilies bloom in orange clusters; lamb's-ears form dense mats of silvery leaves with lavender flowers; and coreopsis 'Moonbeam' puts forth creamy yellow flowers.

If you're hooked on creating a Xeriscape garden of your own, United Water suggests taking into consideration your land's sun exposure, relationship to buildings, slopes, plant groupings, and how the yard is used. Also, condition the soil by mixing in compost, peat moss, or manure to help retain moisture and encourage healthy root growth.

Drought-tolerant plants should be selected for this type of garden. They come in many forms, ranging from colorful flowers and ground covers, to trees and shrubs. Gardeners are also advised to choose drought-tolerant grasses, such as perennial ryes mixed with bluegrass, since these need little water and tolerate foot traffic. Tall fescue grows well in the sun, while fine fescue works best in partly shady areas. Remember to water before 9 AM, never on a windy day; and to use mulch to reduce water evaporation, stop weed growth, maintain even soil temperature, and slow erosion.

After the initial preparation, Xeriscape gardening requires a lot less work than does a traditional garden, although no gardener can escape the chores of weeding, pruning, and fertilizing. To find out how to plan your own water conservation garden, ask for the brochure on Xeriscape gardening, available from the Hackensack Water Company. For further information on Xeriscape gardening, contact corporate headquarters (201-767-9300) or call the Rutgers Cooperative Extension Service (732-699-6162).

NOTE: A short path leads from the garden area to a pond that's frequented by ducks and geese. It's a pleasant place to sit and observe. If you'd like to stretch your legs, cross the road and walk the path circling Oradell Reservoir.

5
Washington Spring Garden

LOCATION ❧ Bergen County
Van Saun County Park
Forest Avenue, Paramus 07652
201-646-2680

GARDEN SIZE ❧ ½ acre

ADMISSION ❧ No charge

WHEN TO VISIT ❧ Daily 9 AM–dusk, year-round. Peak bloom for wildflowers, azaleas, and rhododendrons is from late April through May.

HIGHLIGHTS ❧ Historic spring; azalea banks, tulip beds, dogwood grove, and rhododendrons. In the park, within walking distance of the garden, are a children's zoo, ballfields, shuffleboard courts, and tennis courts.

FACILITIES ❧ Rest room and drinking water

EVENTS ❧ Band concerts in the park. Call for schedule.

I followed the sound of water and came to Washington Spring. Although I couldn't drink from it, as General George Washington did while reviewing his troops here on September 13, 1780, I didn't mind—not when there was so much beauty surrounding the spring.

In 1962, the Bergen County Park Commission created a half-acre garden around this historic spring on the edge of Van Saun Park. In addition to planting dogwoods, azaleas, and tulips, they added a lovely rustic footbridge, paths, benches, and rail fences. Through the years, Washington Spring Garden has attracted many visitors, who come to see not only the famous spring, site of many skirmishes during the Revolutionary War, but also the beautiful, pocket-sized garden.

Come in April when the tulips and daffodils appear. Return in May for the fantastic azalea, mountain laurel, and rhododendron display in vibrant pinks, purples, and oranges. June is special, too: That's when the daylilies and annuals make an appearance. Cool off while sitting on a bench beneath a towering sycamore, sweet gum, or tulip tree, listen to the water's melody as it flows beneath the bridge, and watch the birds as they visit their favorite flowers throughout the summer.

NOTE: Picnicking is allowed in the park.

6

Davis Johnson Memorial Park and Gardens

LOCATION ❧ Bergen County
137 Engle Street
Tenafly 07670
201-569-7275

GARDEN SIZE ❧ 7.5 acres

ADMISSION ❧ No charge

WHEN TO VISIT ❧ Dawn to dusk daily

HIGHLIGHTS ❧ Outstanding rose garden and beech tree collection

FACILITIES ❧ Rest room, benches, partially handicapped-accessible

Established in 1975, this lovely park is particularly magnificent during spring, for that's when thousands of daffodils, tulips, and grape hyacinths are in bloom and dozens of trees are in bud. During July and August, the understory is filled with salvia, daylilies, asters, marigolds and impatiens, while fall is the height of the chrysanthemum display, and the collection of elegant beeches—including the copper, European, three-colored, yellow, and weeping—plus tall tulip trees and maples are showing off their brilliant foliage. There is also a fine collection of firs and rare dwarf conifers.

Of particular note is the Jack Lissemore Rose Garden, which occupies a 100-foot square area within the park. One of approximately 130 gardens in the country accredited by the American Rose Society, it was named for a Tenafly resident who patented the 'Ronda' rose. The garden contains hundreds of roses, including hybrid teas, floribundas, grandifloras, and the spreading varieties. It also displays annual winners chosen by the American Rose Society, which are then donated to the park.

Previously, a mansion occupied these grounds. When its owners died, a builder bought the property and proposed erecting six houses on the site. However, thanks to local residents who formed a land conservancy group and raised a loud enough protest, town officials were encouraged to purchase the property. They then turned it into a park, maintained by the Tenafly Parks Department, to be enjoyed by both Tenafly residents and visitors alike.

7

Backyard Habitat Garden at Flat Rock Brook Nature Center

LOCATION ❧ Bergen County
443 Van Nostrand Avenue
Englewood 07631
201-567-1265

GARDEN SIZE ❧ 4 acres

ADMISSION ❧ No charge

WHEN TO VISIT ❧ *Garden:* Dawn to dusk daily. *Center:* Daily, 9–5.

HIGHLIGHTS ❧ Showcase of native trees, shrubs, and perennials; abundant wildlife; interpretive signs, interpretive center; sitting area next to pond

FACILITIES ❧ Special-needs boardwalk, rest area, picnic facilities; rest room and drinking water in the Center for Environmental Study

EVENTS ❧ Nature Day, environmental festival, plant sale. Call for dates.

In 1993, the Englewood Garden Club won the Garden Club of America's prestigious Founders' Fund Award. With 189 garden clubs competing nationally, it wasn't easy. The winning proposal was for a backyard habitat garden that would use only native plantings with the intention of attracting wildlife, saving water, and reducing pesticide use.

Flat Rock Brook Nature Center is an area covering 150 acres of unspoiled land; it features 180-million-year-old volcanic bedrock formations, wetlands, ponds, a cascading stream, meadows, quarry cliffs, and native ground cover affording shelter for a variety of wildlife. It is here that the 4-acre backyard habitat garden was built.

Bee on bee balm at the Backyard Habitat Garden

The garden was completed in three stages to allow for ecological balance as new seedlings took root. Now, thanks to volunteers and club members, visitors can enjoy this unique and educational sanctuary. Various demonstration areas include an attractive gazebo where native species provide food and shelter for wildlife. These natives include tall grass species, rudbeckia, goldenrod, winterberry, and cardinal flower. During the fall you'll see bumble bees and a variety of butterflies.

From the benches overlooking the pond, you might spot wood ducks, hooded mergansers, and spotted sandpipers. Early in spring, orioles nest in the cottonwood. Black-crowned night herons, box turtles, muskrats, and a number of warblers are among the birds and animals that frequent the area.

Stretch your legs along the boardwalk, especially during spring, when an abundance of hardy native perennial wildflowers and trees are in bloom, such as bloodroot, Solomon's seal, mayapple, Virginia bluebell, and dogwood. Rushes, sedges, and other vegetation indigenous to wetlands can be found along the stream, and if you're fortunate, you might spot an opossum, a very small white-footed mouse, or the short-tailed shrew. Occasionally, red fox and white-tailed deer wander into view.

This is also a birdwatcher's paradise; more than 175 species of birds have been recorded here. During winter months, resident black-capped chickadees, tufted titmice, and downy woodpeckers visit the feeders, and nesting birds include the red-bellied woodpecker, American robin, ovenbird, and rufous-sided towhee. You'll love their music even if you don't see them.

NOTE: Plan enough time to explore the rest of the sanctuary. The 3.5 miles of easy, self-guiding trails through dense forest will take you past large, flat rocks and eventually to Macfadden Pond and the Mystery Bridge (so named because none of the locals saw it under construction). Picnic facilities, including tables, benches, grills, swings, and rest rooms, are available 10 minutes away on Jones Road. Check the map in the garden gazebo for the best way to drive or walk there.

8

Lost Brook Preserve

LOCATION ❧ Bergen County
Tenafly Nature Center
313 Hudson Avenue
Tenafly 07670
201-568-6093

GARDEN SIZE ❧ Approximately 380 acres

ADMISSION ❧ No charge

WHEN TO VISIT ❧ *Trail:* Dawn to dusk; parking lot closes at 5 pm.
Visitor Center: Monday 1–5; Tuesday through
Saturday 9–5, Sunday 10–5, closed holidays.

HIGHLIGHTS ❧ Hundreds of species of plants, trees, and animals;
unusual rock formations

FACILITIES ❧ Rest rooms and water at Visitor Center; natural
history library

EVENTS ❧ Summer classes for children, field trips,
educational programs for children and adults,
campfire evenings. Write for a schedule.

Located in the midst of a busy community, this all-season sanctuary is guaranteed to erase everyday stresses. Stop in at the visitor center first. Here you can find live animals, a touch-table with interactive displays, a library filled with natural history books, and a small gift shop loaded with unique bird feeders and interesting nature books. Before heading outdoors, ask the naturalist for a free trail map.

If the day is sunny, spend a while checking out Pfister's Pond, for you might be lucky enough to spot a northern water snake, a turtle lazing atop a floating branch, or a dragonfly. The aquatic buttonbush, found around the perimeter of the pond, bursts open with 1-inch flower clusters each spring, while in the swampy areas, the spike-shaped flowers of the sweet pepperbush bloom throughout the summer.

From spring through fall, the woods are aglow with a profusion of wildflowers and shrubs, including a lush display of azalea and rhododendron in May and June; ferns that spring to life as early as April; and jewelweed, also know as touch-me-not because the slipper-shaped seedpods burst open at the slightest touch.

Any one of the six trails that meader through the preserve is satisfying, for both the wet and dry areas support a huge variety of trees. The sweetgums, found in the wetter areas, sport spiky ball-shaped fruits, star-shaped leaves, and corky branches and twigs. They are named for the aroma and taste of the resin that the trees release from cuts in their bark. A double-trunked tulip tree can be found about 1.5 miles along the Little-Chism Trail. Also know as the yellow poplar, tulip magnolia, tulip poplar, and whitewood, this specimen also loves moist areas. In May and June it bears beautiful six-petaled yellowish green flowers, each marked in orange at the base. The tulip tree is capable of growing up to 200 feet, and is, according to the Forest Resource Education Center, the tallest growing tree in New Jersey.

Even in the dead of winter, the yellow leaves of the beech tree stubbornly cling to its branches and tremble in the slightest breeze. Capable of reaching 80 feet tall, this native tree produces a canopy so thick that only its own shade-tolerant seedlings can grow beneath it. Wildlife love the sweet nuts the beech produces, and the wood is highly prized for producing flooring, furniture, woodenware, and railroad ties. The shagbark hickory, with long shaggy plates of bark that peel off in rough strips, also makes an appearance in these woods. This outstanding tree often grows to 120 feet tall, bears a delicious nut, and supplies the hard, strong wood used in making sporting goods, for tool handles, and for smoking meat.

The yellow-blazed Allison Trail eventually leads to Green Brook, a wonderful place to spot common woodland creatures, but unless the southern flying squirrel pokes its head out from a tree hole, chances are slim you'll see it during daylight hours. In the flat areas, the Eastern cottontail rabbit can often be seen munching the grass; you might also see woodchuck; white-tailed deer; and, towards dusk, the brown bat.

If you're a bird watcher, you're in for a special treat, especially during the migration periods. More than 175 different species of birds have been recorded here. In May, watch for warblers, thrushes, orioles, grosbeaks, waxwings, and tanagers. As the birds fly south in the fall, red-tailed and sharp-shinned hawks stop by. And during winter, the great horned owl, saw-whet owl, and screech owl hang out in these woods.

9

Dey Mansion Gardens

LOCATION ❧ Passaic County
199 Totowa Road
Wayne 07470
973-696-1776

GARDEN SIZE ❧ Pocket-sized

ADMISSION ❧ No charge

WHEN TO VISIT ❧ *Garden:* Dawn to dusk daily. *House:* Wednesday, Thursday and Friday, 1–4; Saturday and Sunday, 10–noon and 1–4.

HIGHLIGHTS ❧ Knot garden, vast park; historic mansion

FACILITIES ❧ Rest room, benches, picnic tables; handicapped-accessible. The gardens are within Preakness Valley Park, which features a jogging trail and 36-hole golf course.

EVENTS ❧ Annual Revolutionary War Encampment, craft demonstrations, bread baking, quilting, candlemaking. Call for a schedule of these and other events.

Dey Mansion, a Georgian-style mansion built in the 1740s by Dirck Dey, served as George Washington's headquarters in 1780. It was purchased by the Passaic County Parks Commission in 1930, turned into a museum in 1934, and is now part of Preakness Valley Park.

Behind the mansion is a lovely, well-maintained knot garden designed and planted in 1991 by the Riverview Garden Club. According to Beverly Lichtenstein, the club's chairperson, formal gardens like this were common during the Colonial era. She notes that "they were meant to be looked down upon from people's windows so that the intricacies of the knot formation could be appreciated." However, the garden is still attractive when viewed from eye level.

The Colonial-era formal knot garden at Dey Mansion Gardens

As you approach the garden, you'll see an arbor adorned with pretty pink clematis. Just ahead, a beautiful brick pathway, laid by Wayne Township's Eagle Scout Troop 134, leads through the knot garden laid out with red and gold barberry, Japanese holly, and boxwood. Between the front and rear knot gardens sit two stone benches and a huge urn planted with ivy and a small evergreen. An arrangement of pink tree peonies that are boxed in with yews is in either corner of the garden.

Master Gardeners have recently added a striking array of perennials, as well as annual plantings of dusty millers, pansies, begonias, and geraniums in the rear of the garden, where there's also an unusual sundial.

Bring lunch, choose a bench, and relax while gazing out at the garden. Then check out the tall evergreens surrounding the mansion. If you're here during spring, you'll enjoy the fragrant stands of old lilac. Plan on taking a tour of this charming mansion, too. A well, beautifully planted with begonia, ivy, and hosta by members of the Riverview Garden Club, sits near the front entrance. Inside, you'll see the Great Hall, where Washington wrote more than 700 letters while using this as his office; furniture original to that period; a travel box for wigs (the puffier the wig, the more money a man supposedly had); and in the attic, a saber and gun display from the Civil War.

10

Hammond Wildflower Trail at Tourne Park

LOCATION ❧ Morris County
Tourne County Park
McCaffrey Lane
Boonton 07962
973-326-7600

GARDEN SIZE ❧ 545 acres

ADMISSION ❧ No charge

WHEN TO VISIT ❧ Daily, 8 AM–dusk

HIGHLIGHTS ❧ Over 200 wildflowers and shrubs, more than 25 species of ferns

FACILITIES ❧ Rest room, water, public telephone, bicycle rack, picnic tables, hiking trails

This park, which rambles up and down over hills strewn with huge granite boulders, is one of the Garden State's gems. Here, over 200 wildflowers and shrubs, more than 25 species of ferns native to the eastern United States, and hundreds of white oaks, maples, beeches, and hemlocks can be admired. The park is especially attractive in spring, when the Emilie K. Hammond Wildflower Trail is aglow with blossoms in every shape and color.

The Rockaway Valley Garden Club, under the direction of botanist Emilie K. Hammond, for whom the trail is named, organized and identified the huge variety of wildflowers found within the park. Later, the Garden Club of Mountain Lakes joined in the effort to maintain the plantings, which grow in varied terrain along a 1-mile stretch of winding paths.

You reach the Wildflower Trail by entering the park at Powerville Road. Purple violets, Robin's plantain, Dutchman's-breeches, bluebells, and Jacob's ladder can be found alongside the trail before it branches off to the Brookside or Overlook Trail. Take the right fork onto the Brookside Trail to hear gurgling water and search the low boggy areas for skunk cabbage, which pokes up as early as February. Spring awakens the goldenseal, used as a curative during the 17th and 18th centuries; pink lady's slipper, a member of the orchid family; and Oconee bells, a bell-shaped flower discovered in the North Carolina mountains in 1788.

Follow the spicy scent of trailing arbutus a short distance ahead. According to legend, the Pilgrims found this flower in the woods after a freezing winter, and seeing it filled them with hope and joy. In the wooded area, before you decide whether to take the Swamp or the Fern Walk Trail, you'll find abundant Canada anemone, trillium, and a huge beech tree. Shooting star, blue phlox, bleeding heart, columbine, hepatica, and Maidenhair, Christmas, and Interrupted ferns, all thrive along the Fern Walk Trail. The Swamp Trail is home to hundreds of Cardinal flowers, marsh marigolds, early buttercups, trout lilies, and mayapples. Trillium Walk is spectacular during spring, when it's awash in blooming toad trillium, snow trillium, dwarf white trillium, and many other varieties.

Don't leave without exploring the rest of this glorious park, for after huffing and puffing your way uphill past impressive woods, you'll be rewarded with a panoramic view of Manhattan's skyline. The name *Tourne* comes from the Dutch word meaning "lookout" or "mountain." Tourne Park is the only remaining undeveloped fragment of the Great Boonton Tract, which had been purchased by David Ogden, Colonial attorney-general of New Jersey in 1759. According to park literature, "Clarence Addington DeCamp (1859–1948) inherited and acquired during his lifetime much of the land now preserved as Tourne County Park. Using hand tools and levers, he built two roads to the top of the Tourne and encouraged the citizenry to enjoy the forests and fields with him, thereby becoming one of the first conservationists in Morris County."

Besides the fabulous view, there's also an incredible glacial erratic, known as the Mouse Cradle Balancing Rock, resting on the southwestern summit of the Tourne. Balanced on two points of ledge rock and a hidden wedge stone, this huge rock is estimated to weigh 54 tons. It got its name in 1897 when DeCamp discovered a mouse nest in a cleft of the rock!

NOTE: Dogs and bicycles are not permitted along the wildflower trail.

Volunteer Gladys Lockyer tending the Waterloo Village Herb Garden

11
Waterloo Village Gardens

LOCATION ❦ Sussex County
Waterloo Village
Off Route 80, exit 25, and follow signs
Stanhope 07874
973-347-0900

GARDEN SIZE ❦ Approximately 10 acres for all the gardens

ADMISSION ❦ Fee

WHEN TO VISIT ❦ Wednesday through Sunday 10–6, mid-April through mid-November

HIGHLIGHTS ❦ Herb, perennial, and vegetable gardens

FACILITIES ❦ Rest room, water, benches, handicapped-accessible garden areas

EVENTS ❦ Talks; Oktoberfest and Apple Festival each October. Call for a schedule of these and many other events.

Time stands still at Waterloo Village, where blacksmiths hammer away over a fire, a chandler makes hand-dipped candles, and a weaver plies a colonial loom.

Located in a natural setting along the banks of the Musconetcong River, and steeped in American history dating back to the Revolutionary era, Waterloo Village is peaceful and charming. While strolling past costumed guides, visitors can see a gristmill that has withstood the years. It stands along a segment of the Morris Canal with its inclined plane still in place. Notice also the mule bridge and guard lock that made Waterloo a major canal port in 1831. Here, too, you can explore a re-created 400-year-old Lenape village, with its longhouse, dugout canoes, tools and crafts; or stock up on original pottery and made-on-site brooms at the General Store; watch artisans demonstrate early cloth-making at the Weaving Barn; observe historical reenactments throughout the village;

or listen to the swapping of stories at the Towpath Tavern.

In the Apothecary and Herb-Drying Room, Gladys Lockyer recounts how herbal cures and natural remedies were obtained from medicinal herbs planted outside most village homes. Lockyer, a volunteer in her eighties who's worked here for years, is always happy to answer questions and describe how herbs were used as cures for colds, sore throats, and minor afflictions. In the drying room, herbs are hung in the dark upside down from the ceiling because in this way, notes Lockyer, they hold their color better and lose all their pollen after they're dried.

The Herb Garden, located outside the Apothecary, is chock-full of scented plants and many varieties of thyme. "This is more than an old-fashioned herb garden," says Lockyer, "since, besides the perennials, it has large clumps of lavender growing inside the diamond-shaped section, and lots of onions."

The Perennial Garden at the Canal Museum boasts an attractive grapevine, weigela, Russian lavender, yarrow, peonies, mint, catnip, and more, and is shaded by a beautiful cherry tree and a tall locust. Topiary junipers are planted in huge pots, and perhaps the most outstanding flowers in this garden are the gigantic hibiscus. Behind the main office, a circular garden is filled with a mixture of vegetables and over 2,000 colorful annuals, all reachable via a path running through the center. Sunglasses are advisable when admiring the Salvia Garden, for the over 1,800 brilliant specimens planted here are truly dazzling when the sun is shining.

12
Merrill Creek Reservoir Butterfly and Hummingbird Garden

LOCATION ❧ Warren County
Merrill Creek Reservoir
116 Montana Road
Washington 07882
908-454-1213

GARDEN SIZE ❧ Pocket-sized

ADMISSION ❧ No charge

WHEN TO VISIT ❧ *Garden:* Dawn to dusk daily, year-round. The best time is during July and August, when butterflies and hummingbirds visit. *Visitors Center:* Daily 9–5; closed holidays.

HIGHLIGHTS ❧ Nearby hiking trails, fishing, boating, birding

FACILITIES ❧ Rest room and water inside visitors center; portable toilets at boat ramp

People from all over the state are drawn to Merrill Creek Reservoir. They come to fish, photograph, cross-country ski, observe wildlife, bird-watch, and hike the well-maintained trails that meander through woods, fields, and wetlands. Summer visitors come to admire the Butterfly and Hummingbird Garden, opened in 1990, which draws an astonishing number of hummingbirds, butterflies, bees, and other beneficial insects.

The plantings in this small, stunning garden—located behind the modern visitors center—were carefully chosen for their value in attracting wildlife. Some boast brightly colored flowers, others are rich in nectar, and a few, such as dill, parsley, and milkweed, have foliage that

Merrill Creek Reservoir Butterfly and Hummingbird Garden

supply the necessary food for caterpillars. A feeder filled with sugar water is placed in the garden early in the season to supplement the diet of the ruby-throated hummingbird. However, once the plantings mature, the feeder is no longer necessary.

Many butterflies require two species of plants to complete their life cycle: one for the larvae or caterpillar stage, and another for the nectar-loving adult butterfly stage. For example, while the caterpillar of the black swallowtail dines on parsley and dill, the adult swallowtail butterfly prefers butterfly weed. Both caterpillars and adults enjoy the thistle, clover, and Queen Anne's lace found in the unmowed areas surrounding the garden.

You'll find butterflies hovering over the birdbath, as well as the buddleia (butterfly bush), wild bergamot, mountain mint, blue lobelia, and obedient plant. The obedient plant, which is named for its ability to maintain whatever position it is bent into, bursts into bloom in late summer and spreads very quickly.

If you station yourself near the bee balm, a tall plant with a minty scent and clusters of hooded flowers, or the butterfly weed, a fragrant specimen sporting tiny, brilliant orange flowers, you'll be able to watch some of the butterflies' flight patterns, which vary from species to species depending on whether they're out hunting for food, a mate, or a place to lay their eggs.

Before leaving, stop in at the visitors center to learn why and how the Merrill Creek Reservoir was situated atop Scott Mountain, and how the stored water is released to the Delaware River during periods of low flow and times of drought. Then, stretch your legs over one of the beautiful trails or rest on one of the garden benches.

13
Pequest Butterfly Garden

LOCATION ❧ Warren County
Off Route 46, east of the Route 31 junction
Pequest 07863
908-637-4125

GARDEN SIZE ❧ Less than ¼ acre

ADMISSION ❧ No charge

WHEN TO VISIT ❧ *Garden:* Dawn to dusk daily, year-round. *Visitors Center:* Open daily 10–4, year-round except holidays.

HIGHLIGHTS ❧ Butterfly garden; adjacent Trout Hatchery and Natural Resource Education Center

FACILITIES ❧ Rest room and drinking water inside the Education Center building; handicapped-accessible

EVENTS ❧ Special weekend nature programs and fishing lessons April through October in the Education Center

This tiny garden is specifically designed for butterflies: The many mourning cloaks, fiery skippers, gray hairstreaks, painted ladies, black swallowtails, Eastern tiger swallowtails, and monarchs it attracts put on a glorious show. Come any time from late spring through late fall, bring lots of film, and both a close-up and a telephoto lens. Since butterflies see in color and are sensitive to the ultraviolet range of light, it's best to heed Robert Michael Pyle's advice in his book *Handbook for Butterfly Watchers:* Wear drab clothing so as not to distract them, and move with "stealth, deliberation, and fluidity."

Butterflies play an important role in pollination: As they feed on nectar, they carry pollen on their bodies from one flower to another. Notice that some butterfly species head to the milkweed, others choose flowers with large petals to perch on while feeding, and still others flutter around blossoms with vivid colors.

Two types of food plants grow in this garden: one for the selective larva (caterpillar), the other for the nectar-loving adult (butterfly). In addition to cultivated plants such as alyssum, candytuft, marigold, salvia, zinnia, catnip, phlox, primrose, and columbine, an abundance of wild vegetation surrounds the garden. Many plants we consider commonplace weeds—including milkweed, thistle, clover, and Queen Anne's lace—are devoured by caterpillars and butterflies.

A shallow dish of wet sand placed in a sunny location serves as a "puddling station." Here butterflies, which do not drink from open water, can "puddle," or remove water from the moist sand.

You'll probably notice butterflies heading to and coming from nearby trees, shrubs, and weeds. These provide windbreaks and hiding places so they can escape from birds and other predators. There's also a hibernation box; it's been placed for the mourning cloaks, and enables them to hibernate in the adult stage until they emerge from semidormancy in spring.

NOTE: Plan on exploring the visitors center. There you can view a short video describing how fish eggs are taken from the adjacent hatchery's own brood stock and how the brooks and streams are stocked with fish raised here; examine hands-on exhibits that describe various aspects of the state's wildlife and natural resources; take a self-guided tour of the grounds, and stopping at the observation deck for a close-up look at the raceways where the trout are reared from fingerling to stocking size. You can also stretch your legs along one of the surrounding short nature trails.

14
Well-Sweep Herb Farm

LOCATION ❧ Warren County
205 Mount Bethel Road (near Route 57)
Port Murray 07865
908-852-5390

GARDEN SIZE ❧ Approximately ½ acre

ADMISSION ❧ No charge

WHEN TO VISIT ❧ Monday 1–5; Tuesday through Saturday 9:30–5;
closed Sundays and holidays. Call to confirm
hours.

HIGHLIGHTS ❧ Educational herb garden, medicinal herb garden,
English knot garden, perennials; farm animals;
and a huge variety of plants for sale

FACILITIES ❧ Rest room, drinking water, gift shop

EVENTS ❧ Open House in June and September; Christmas
shop; craft classes, lectures, slide shows,
exhibitions. Call for hours.

Well-Sweep Herb Farm is home to one of the largest collections of herbs in the country. The beautiful half-acre garden boasts a variety of herbs, including 36 types of basil, 60 different lavenders, 80 varieties of thyme, rosemary topiary standards, and more than 100 scented geraniums in the knot garden. Visitors will also find lovely tiny gardens scattered about with an assortment of beautiful flowers.

Herbs, planted through the ages for their medicinal and culinary value, have special meaning for Cyrus Hyde, owner of Well-Sweep Herb Farm. Hyde's mother often treated his family with herbal remedies passed down from his great-great-great-grandmother, who fed and nursed men in George Washington's army. In gratitude for her help, Washington presented her with a pair of silver knee buckles, one of which is still in Cyrus Hyde's possession.

To fulfill his lifelong interest in herbs, Hyde and his wife, Louise, purchased the farm in 1967. Hyde, a collector of unusual plants from around the world, immediately began raising herbs around their house despite the fact that the soil was heavy clay. He set to work improving the land, and after years of plowing, fertilizing, and planting, he was rewarded for his labors with this beautiful garden.

Planted around the house you'll find feverfew, used for migraine headaches; rose geranium, great in apple jelly; summer savory, delicious in beans; tansy, said to keep away ants when it's dried; apple sage, treasured for its fragrant aroma on breezy evenings; garlic chives, an essential ingredient in most Chinese stir-frying; and chervil, similar in taste to parsley. You'll also find borage, known for its cucumber flavor and pretty, star-shaped flowers used to decorate drinks and cakes; rosemary, good on lamb, chicken, and pork; lovage, stronger in flavor than celery and excellent in potato salad; miniature impatiens, used as a border; rosebud impatiens; and Spanish peppermint, twining around an ornamental bell. Myrtle, traditionally used in Polish bridal wreaths, is abundant on the grounds, along with tea and coffee plants.

The property was named after the old stone well in front of the house. In earlier times, a family depended on hand-drawn well water for its drinking and bathing needs, and the "well-sweep," which is exactly like the one Hyde used as a child, was designed to lighten the load. Generally, a tall tree is used as the base of a well-sweep, and it has to be Y-shaped at one end. A second, longer tree branch, known as the "sweep," is placed in the Y of the base at an angle to the well, thus forming a lever. To retrieve water from the well, the bucket is lowered by raising the sweep and, once filled, the bucket is raised by allowing the heavy sweep to lower slowly to the ground.

NOTE: The gift shop is filled with irresistible herbs, seeds, standards, books, and other items. Ask for a catalog listing the hundreds of herbs and plants available by mail. Bring a picnic lunch to enjoy at the farm, which is nestled in the scenic hills of Warren County; the nearest restaurant is about 15 minutes away in Washington.

15
Willowwood Arboretum

LOCATION ❧ Morris County
Longview Road
Chester Township 07930
973-326-7600

GARDEN SIZE ❧ 130 acres

ADMISSION ❧ No charge

WHEN TO VISIT ❧ Dawn to dusk daily, year-round

HIGHLIGHTS ❧ Formal gardens, thousands of native and exotic plants, a superb dawn redwood, collections of magnolias, hollies, cherries, lilacs, and conifers

EVENTS ❧ Educational seminars; call for dates and times

Visitors are free to stroll year-round in Willowwood Arboretum, a 130-acre wonderland of trees with 3,500 species of native and exotic plants. In this undisturbed forest you'll find 35 kinds of oak, 50 varieties of maple, 110 willow species from all over the Northern Hemisphere, and a superb dawn redwood—raised from a 3-foot-tall seedling sent from Princeton in 1948—that's now over 80 feet high. Wildflowers and ferns burst open each spring, along with lilacs, magnolias, hollies, and cherries against a backdrop of conifers.

In 1908, Henry and Robert Tubbs decided to make this property, then known as Paradise Farm, their permanent country home. Except for the thick chestnut and oak woods remaining on the western hill, the property had been used as pastureland and was a working farm from the early 1700s. Because huge weeping willows dominated the approach to the house, the name was changed to Willowbrook Farm. Those early trees are long gone, except for one 30-foot-tall descendant that still grows by the brook. The original single-species collection has been expanded through the years and now includes about 110 species of shrub and tree willows from around the world.

Over the course of 50 years, the Tubbs brothers planted approximately 20,000 conifers, including pines, spruces, and larches. To protect their work, they stipulated in their will that the property be maintained after their deaths as an arboretum and wildlife preserve. It was established as a private arboretum in 1950 and remained under the proprietorship of Rutgers, the State University, from 1967 until 1980, when it officially became a unit of the Morris County Parks Department.

The house, built in 1792, dominates two small formal gardens, with informal paths leading through open areas and woodland. Throughout the property you'll see hydrangeas, honeysuckles, spireas, forsythias, lilacs, roses, peonies, and hostas that were given to the brothers as gifts. You'll also see specimens that Robert Tubbs purchased in New York markets and around the world, including Chinese silk trees, Chinese lace-bark pine, 'Waterlily' magnolia, and Chinese house lemon.

Pick up a trail guide from the box in the parking area and explore the short, easy trail that winds around the property. The barn at the beginning of the trail, constructed in the 1790s using local Roxbury pudding stone, is used today as a horticultural education center. A collection of lilacs, including many of the more unusual species and hybrids, grows near the wooden barn; peak flowering time is from late April through May. A golden-rain tree at trail marker 5 boasts bright yellow flowers in July; they turn into Japanese-lantern-like pods that cling to the tree for months after.

See how many species you can identify in the spectacular stand of oaks from all over the world. The turkey oak, for instance, has an attractive acorn with fringed scales on the cup. A short distance away, at stop 10, is a hill cherry, known for its single pale pink flowers each spring. During fall, the sassafras—famous for having leaves of three different shapes on one tree—turns a brilliant orange. A number of magnolias are scattered along the woodland area, and at stop 15, the slow-growing sapphire berry shrub makes its presence known in late spring when it displays panicles of fragrant white flowers. Return during fall to see its bright ultramarine fruits.

Ferns thrive in the moist areas, dominated by the ostrich fern, which often reaches a height of 5 feet or more. The interrupted fern, identified by fertile spore-bearing fronds, is the first to uncoil in the spring. Just before the stone bridge, constructed in 1952 of stones gathered from nearby fencerows, is the native snowbell, which bears nodding clusters of white flowers in spring. From May through June, the right side of the path is covered with flowering Japanese primrose ranging from white and pale pink to magenta.

Those stumpy projections rising above the ground at stop 23 are the "knees" of the bald cypress trees that tower overhead. The knees—actually the roots—serve to anchor the trees in the soft mud. Continue along the stepping-stones to the pool on the other side to see the Cypress Pool Garden, where bald cypress, Hinoki cypress, moss cypress, and Japanese maples grow.

A lush stand of bamboo grows near the end of the trail. On a breezy day, take a moment to stand still and listen to the wonderful music as the plants gently sway against each other.

16

Phoenix House Garden

LOCATION ❧ Morris County
Mendham Municipal Building
Main Street and Hilltop Road
Mendham 07945
973-543-7152

GARDEN SIZE ❧ Less than ¼ acre

ADMISSION ❧ No charge

WHEN TO VISIT ❧ *Garden:* Dawn to dusk daily, year-round. *Phoenix House:* Open Monday through Friday, 9–4:30.

FACILITIES ❧ Rest room inside Phoenix House; picnicking allowed in the garden

EVENTS ❧ Annual plant sale. Call for date.

This charming garden, which stands adjacent to historic Phoenix House, is a treasure, thanks to the efforts of the Mendham Garden Club.

Marjorie M. Davidson, a member since 1956, recalls that the club was organized in 1932 "by a group of concerned women to beautify the grounds, which until that time had been a town eyesore filled with weeds, broken bits of crockery, and old shoes. They met the challenge with vigor and talent, carting in fresh soil and plants to conform with the 19th-century English-style design plan drawn by Martha Brooks Hutchinson, a prominent architect."

Although its origins are unknown, garden club members note that in the early 1800s William Phoenix acquired Phoenix Hall, a classic Federal-style building completed in 1806; the property, run as an inn and tavern, remained in his family for 100 years. Known as the Phoenix Hotel Road House, it was a popular stopping place for people traveling through on what is now Highway 24.

The house slowly deteriorated until 16 local residents purchased it in 1919. By the time Senator Arthur Whitney acquired the property in

1923, it had passed through many hands and served as a meeting place, tearoom, dress shop, and antiques shop. In 1938, when Whitney donated the property to the people of Mendham, it became the official municipal offices for the Borough of Mendham.

Today, the outside of the handsome building looks basically as it did when it was first erected, except for a Greek Revival porch that was added in the mid-19th century. And although no record of its original interior has been found, the restoration is compatible with the Federal architecture of the building. A mural in the front hall depicts Mendham Village in the early 1800s, and antiques found in the attic have been restored and are now on view.

While most visitors come to this quaint town to visit its antiques and gift shops, the lucky few who wander into the garden are taken by its beauty. Dedicated to the memory of Ella W. Mockridge, founder and first president of the Mendham Garden Club, the garden consists of seven sections, each outlined with ivy. Plantings include cosmos, a tall, pink-flowered annual with lacy foliage; blue salvia, which emits a glow late in the day; tall, lush snapdragons, and sweet-smelling petunia. Lovely shade trees enclose the area, and curved fieldstone benches have been thoughtfully placed at strategic viewing points. The espaliered crab apple trees that cling to the stucco wall of Phoenix House are particularly beautiful in spring, when the buds burst open; later in the season, the flaming red cardinal flower attracts the attention of visitors and hummingbirds alike. If you enjoy bird-watching, sit near the unusual slate birdbaths that are placed at ground level and watch the birds compete for a turn to splash.

If possible, plan for a Tuesday morning visit; that's when garden club members plant and prune.

17
Wick Kitchen Herb Garden and Farm

LOCATION ❧ Morris County
Morristown National Historic Park /
Jockey Hollow Section
Tempe Wick and Jockey Hollow Roads
Harding Township 07940
973-539-2085

GARDEN SIZE ❧ Less than 1 acre

ADMISSION ❧ No charge

WHEN TO VISIT ❧ Daily 9–5

HIGHLIGHTS ❧ 18th-century herb and vegetable garden and farmhouse

FACILITIES ❧ Rest room

EVENTS ❧ Encampment re-enactment and other celebrations. Call for a schedule.

The Wick Kitchen Herb Garden and Farm offers a glimpse of a prosperous family's property as it appeared in 1777—the same year General George Washington led his weary, starving troops to winter quarters here at Jockey Hollow, 4 miles south of Morristown, after victories at Trenton and Princeton. The Wick Farm is surrounded by 1,000 wooded acres that have been preserved as part of the Morristown National Historic Park.

Henry Wick and his brother-in-law, Nathaniel Cooper, acquired this land in 1746. Two years later, after purchasing Cooper's share, Wick built a Cape Cod-style farmhouse for his wife and four children. Furnishings similar to those used in the second and third quarter of the 18th century are represented in the house, which is open for tours; several reconstructed outbuildings stand near the garden and orchard.

Wick Kitchen Herb Garden and Farm

The farm, like the house, is of early New England design. To keep his family supplied with vegetables, seasoning herbs, and simples, or medicinal herbs, Wick planted a kitchen garden alongside his house. Some flowers were grown, for ornamental purposes only. Thanks to the discovery of a 1786 map, the reconstructed garden now stands exactly on the site of the original. Today, the Wick House Kitchen Herb Garden is tended by the National Park Service, in cooperation with the Northern New Jersey Unit of the Herb Society of America, as a demonstration garden for educational and living history purposes.

Wick's garden, like most in colonial times, was orderly. Its rectangular beds were bordered by red and black currants, gooseberry bushes, meadow saffron, and chives. Today, only plants that were available in Wick's time have been added, such as the row of 'Early English' turnips that were grown from seed nurtured by descendants of a New Jersey family for two centuries. A few varieties have changed over time, thanks to horticultural and botanical advances. For example, 'Buttersea' asparagus grew in Wick's day, but is no longer available. However, scarlet runner beans are still harvested today.

The orchard has many fruit trees, including the damson plum, and several varieties of apples, such as Spitzenberg, Russet, Sheepsnose, Golden Rennet, Newtown Pippin, and Rhode Island Greening. The herbs, tended by women in period dress, include Good King Henry, used as a potherb or as an infusion with laxative effects; agrimony, made into tea and spring tonic; anise, a flavoring in breads, cakes, and confections; bugleweed, taken for coughs; leaves of betony, used for ruptures, cramps, snakebite, and headaches; and costmary, used to flavor ale and bring it to a head before the introduction of hops. The flowers of German chamomile were used in tea and as a sedative; meadow saffron root was taken as a gout medicine; the leaves of deadnettle helped stop bleeding; the flowers of golden Marguerite produced a yellow dye; and pennyroyal was an effective mosquito and insect repellent.

NOTE: After visiting the farm, kitchen garden, and farmhouse, don't miss the opportunity to walk one of the many well-marked trails within Morristown National Historic Park.

18

Tunis-Ellicks Parlor Garden

LOCATION ❧ Morris County
Village Road and Millbrook Road
New Vernon 07976
973-539-5918

GARDEN SIZE ❧ Pocket-sized

ADMISSION ❧ No charge

WHEN TO VISIT ❧ *Garden:* Dawn to dusk daily, year-round. *House:*
Hours vary during spring and fall; call for times.

HIGHLIGHTS ❧ Authentic re-creation of an early-1800s parlor
garden; circa-1800 house listed on the National
and State Registers of Historic Places; museum
collection representative of New Jersey farming
in the early 19th century

FACILITIES ❧ Rest room when house is open

EVENTS ❧ Open House and lectures throughout the year.
Call for a schedule.

This small, exquisite garden, planted and maintained by the New Vernon Garden Club since 1978, is an authentic re-creation of the circa-1800 parlor gardens that were popular after the Revolution.

Following the front property line in a triangular corner, and enclosed behind an attractive low picket fence, are small, neat beds containing 120 varieties of herbs, perennials, and shrubs. There isn't any grass to mow; lawnmowers, a high-tech English invention of the 1830s, weren't around yet. Instead, straight paths of river-bottom gravel provide easy access to all the beds. It's believed that Mrs. Tunis, one of the second owners, probably didn't care about the subtleties of color design, so plants have been placed where they would have been most convenient for her to get to them. Therefore, in some sections, tall plants are planted in front of smaller ones.

During May and June, sweet woodruff, dianthus, columbine, and candytuft bloom beneath the shrubs. Later, hollyhock, lupine, evening primrose, and coreopsis add color. Several beds are filled with flowers for drying, cooking, or dyes. The center bed features thyme, scented geraniums, and carnations; the Rose Bed features old-fashioned roses and is bordered by chives and parsley.

One bed is devoted to two special rosebushes, a 'Crested Moss' and a 'De Meaux', while nearby there's an edging of chives, strawberries, and germander. Additional beds include flowers for fragrance, with scented geraniums, rosemary, and lemon verbena; for household use, including comfrey, tansy, and winter savory; and yarrow, salvia, and lady's-mantle for drying. Masses of lemon verbena, rosemary, peppermint, rose geranium, and lavender provide the ingredients for potpourri.

In addition to the numerous old lilacs around the house, you'll find azalea, Washington hawthorn, and winterberry. An ancient maple shades the kitchen dooryard, and a large calycanthus, with dark red strawberry-scented flowers, dominates the southwest corner. Here you'll also see aster, evening primrose, yarrow, sweet woodruff, goldenrod, and fox-glove, in addition to borders of dogwood, boxwood, and periwinkle.

The Tunis-Ellicks House, listed on the National and State Registers of Historic Places, was built for George Mitchell around 1799 and sold to Silas D. Tunis in 1838. In 1978, the decaying house and garden were rescued by a group of concerned citizens who accurately restored it to its present state. A fine example of an East New Jersey farmhouse with three-bay construction, it appears as it did in the early 19th century. The kitchen wing features an authentic Federal mantel; the fireplace and bee-hive oven were restored and are now used for open-hearth cooking demonstrations. The second floor serves as a museum, with a growing collection reflecting the evolution of a town and its residents from colonial days to the present.

Before leaving the grounds, check out the Tramp House. Built by order of the Morris County Board of Freeholders, this circa-1876 structure provided a night's lodging for those homeless wanderers of the post–Civil War depression years. It was moved here in 1988 from its original location in what is now the Great Swamp National Wildlife Refuge. You might also want to follow the straight path leading directly from the western side of the house and garden across the road to get a closer look at the apple tree grove as well as a building that once served as the town's coach and mail stop.

19

Bamboo Brook Gardens

LOCATION ❧ Morris County
Longview Road
Chester Township
973-326-7600

GARDEN SIZE ❧ Approximately 100 acres

ADMISSION ❧ No charge

WHEN TO VISIT ❧ Daily 9 AM–dusk

HIGHLIGHTS ❧ Formal garden with beautiful vistas, fields, a forest, and a series of outdoor areas with formal and naturalistic plantings

FACILITIES ❧ None

EVENTS ❧ Educational classes and occasional concerts. Call for a schedule.

In her book *The Spirit of the Garden*, Martha Brookes Hutcheson wrote, "The garden is not only the exquisite playground of the home but a place of inspiration and promise, of tranquillity and intense personal claim, and we are held and inspired by it." Hutcheson was a graduate of MIT and the second woman in the country to receive training as a landscape architect. In 1911 she and her husband William purchased this property, then known as Merchiston Farm, and immediately began laying out plans for a garden.

As a member of the Society of Landscape Architects, Mrs. Hutcheson was well qualified for this task, having designed gardens for estates in Massachusetts, Long Island, and New Jersey. By 1935, she had transformed the 5-acre area around her house into a formal garden with water features and mature native specimen trees. She remained here until 1959; in 1974, her daughter, Martha Hutcheson Norton, donated the property to the Morris County Parks Commission in memory of her parents. The name of the garden was changed to Bamboo Brook, for the stream that flows through the grounds.

As you face the house, in the center section you can still see part of the original structure, which was built in the 1720s. Although it was originally painted white, Mrs. Hutcheson had the exterior covered with cedar shakes to help it blend in with its natural setting. The front walk is lined with boxwood, and the English yew in this area has been allowed to grow into a small tree. The pineapple above the doorway is a colonial symbol of hospitality; although the house is not open to visitors, you'll feel welcome the moment you set foot on these grounds.

During spring, the circular drive is lined with flowering dogwood. Nearby, a European white birch shows off its distinctive black and white bark, and each autumn it displays brilliant yellow diamond-shaped leaves. Here you'll also see a yellowwood and an American hop horn-beam; it has loose, scaly bark and drooping catkins that appear in April and May, followed by a hoplike fruit loved by bobwhite, deer, and rabbits. You'll also see a tall, graceful Eastern hemlock, a Kentucky coffee tree, and a sweet gum, recognizable by its star-shaped leaves and fall colors of purple, orange, and red.

As you walk along, you'll notice that Mrs. Hutcheson's garden utilizes many classical elements common to both English and Italian gardens: they include pools, stone walls, an interrupted watercourse, and near and far vistas. She also took advantage of the babbling brook that runs through the property and created informal trails leading to the fields, forest, and brook.

Many of the plants are identified by tags, but it's best to bring along wildflower, tree, bird, or butterfly identification books, depending on your interest. There are more than 25 varieties of wildflowers on the grounds, including red baneberry, rue, anemone, columbine, jack-in-the-pulpit, black cohosh, yellow lady's slipper, bleeding heart, wintergreen, bloodroot, and false Solomon's seal. You'll also see many varieties of fern, including maidenhair, marginal wood, spinulose wood, and ostrich and Christmas ferns. The perennial garden area, bordered with old-fashioned flowers such as bleeding heart, phlox, and daylily, leads to a structure originally built as a playhouse for Mrs. Hutcheson's daughter. Now more than 50 years old, it's used by visiting school classes.

Japanese wisteria climbs the stone pillars of an old arbor where tennis players cooled off between games; crab apples, adorned with brilliant blossoms each spring, line the lower garden; and roses and clematis wind around the cedar arbor. The Little House, surrounded by native shrubs and wildflowers, is the site of Mrs. Hutcheson's summer studio, because the brook running beneath it appealed to her sense of romance. There's also a semicircular dipping pool, originally used to catch rainwater for the vegetable garden, and a round reflecting pool.

No matter when you visit, there's something in bloom—columbine raised from seed brought from Germany; rhododendron, fabulous in May; mock orange, sporting white blossoms with an orange fragrance; ornamental rhubarb, grown for its attractive leaves; and witch hazel, which takes on new life in late fall when its bare branches are covered with light yellow blooms. The low-growing weed with variegated leaves you'll see growing throughout the property is known as goutweed or bishop's weed. This European wildflower—sporting tiny white or yellowish flowers in early summer—was brought in by accident on the roots of a woody plant Mrs. Hutcheson had purchased from a nursery; she sued the nursery when she realized that the weed was invading her entire garden!

20
Delbarton Gardens

LOCATION ❧ Morris County
Delbarton School
Mendham Road (Route 24)
Morristown 07960
973-538-3231
GARDEN SIZE ❧ More than 360 acres
ADMISSION ❧ No charge
WHEN TO VISIT ❧ Weekdays 9–5; weekends 9 AM–dusk; guided
garden tours by appointment
HIGHLIGHTS ❧ Lovely Italian garden with statuary, rolling lawn,
and abundant trees and shrubbery
FACILITIES ❧ Rest room when the school is open

Located only 3 miles west of bustling Morristown, this 400-acre woodland campus is the home of Delbarton School, a private day school opened in 1939 by the Benedictine Fathers of Saint Mary's Abbey; it's also a green paradise open to garden lovers.

The campus, adjacent to Jockey Hollow, a national historic park, is accessed by a long, winding driveway that takes you past manicured lawns, ponds filled with ducks and geese, and tall trees stretching their limbs across the road to form a canopy of shade. At the top of the hill stands an impressive mansion designed by Stanford White and built in 1883 by Luther Kountze, an international banker. Used by the Kountze family as their summer residence, Delbarton was named for three of the children, Delancy, Barkley, and Livingston. At that time, the family owned 4,000 acres, but after their deaths, all but approximately 360 acres were sold to the George Washington Association in Morristown for $1 and eventually added to the National Park System.

Stop in at the office for a free, self-guiding brochure before walking to the Italian-style garden. It's filled with the statuary and urns that

Azaleas at Delbarton Gardens

Kountze imported from Italy and Greece. Much of the damage to those on display is the result of our climate and acid rain. Among the sculptures is a monumental Roman marble bust of a goddess, dating to 1 A.D.; an 18th-century Venetian stone figure of Mars; four English marble busts of the evangelists Matthew, Mark, Luke, and John, dating from the second half of the 19th century; and 12 smaller 19th-century Corinthian capitals.

The two-level garden contains a 200-foot-long pergola with wooden latticework on the south side that was specifically built to cast shadows over the flower beds and statues. Since points of view were integral to the design of Italian gardens, the pergola was also situated to give perspective on the geometry of the garden. The walls of the garden are constructed of native white granite, and around the perimeter are specimen magnolia, a honey cherry, red maple, and a red-leafed euonymus.

As you stroll, you'll find many stately trees, including Norway maple, beech, dogwood, and holly, as well as beautiful annuals tended by Father Beatus of the Abbey. If you visit during the winter, you're bound to see dozens of deer and turkey grazing here. Although wonderful to admire, they cause a great deal of damage to the gardens.

The mansion features oak and mahogany paneling, and hand-carved stair rails and wainscoting imported from Europe. The French doors of the living room lead out to a porch overlooking the formal Italian garden.

NOTE: Visitors are welcome to worship services inside the Abbey Church, completed in 1966.

21
Acorn Hall Gardens

LOCATION ❧ Morris County
68 Morris Avenue
Morristown 07960
973-267-3465

GARDEN SIZE ❧ Less than 2 acres

ADMISSION ❧ *Gardens:* No charge. *Mansion tour:* Fee.

WHEN TO VISIT ❧ *Gardens:* Dawn to dusk daily, year-round. *Acorn Hall:* Thursday 11–3; Sunday 1:30–4; closed January, February, and major holidays.

HIGHLIGHTS ❧ Ornate gazebo; old-fashioned roses; ancient trumpet vine; hydrangeas, and peonies; a variety of wildflowers; Acorn Hall

FACILITIES ❧ Rest room when Acorn Hall is open

EVENTS ❧ Holly Walk first weekend in December; changing exhibits; special holiday events. Call for schedule.

In 1971, the Morris County Historical Society moved its headquarters to Acorn Hall, an impressive Italianate mansion built in 1853. That same year, the society asked the Home Garden Club of Morristown to restore the long-neglected grounds surrounding the mansion. Club member Alice Dustan Kollar drew up an elaborate design using only those plants available to gardeners between 1853 and 1888, a period when vast expanses of lawn area were reserved for croquet and natural woodland areas were cherished for their beauty.

From the parking area, walk to the front of the house, where thick beds of myrtle and large boxwood hug the porch. Across the U-shaped driveway is an original hitching post; nearby stands the magnificent red oak, estimated to be about 200 years old, that inspired the mansion's name. Large rhododendron and laurel bushes, planted by the original owner, Dr. John P. Schermerhorn, burst into bloom in spring. A Katsura tree, valued for its fall foliage of yellow, pink, or purple, is planted to the left of the path beside the house.

Toward the back of the mansion, curved areas brimming with hostas and leucothoe, typical of the naturalistic style popular in the Victorian era, surround a flagstone patio. The patio is set with inviting antique metal chairs and benches, where you can sit to admire the vast lawn before strolling to the woodland garden, planted with delicate ferns, wildflowers, and beautiful trees, including a weeping cherry and a smoke bush. Farther along, Concord grapevines climb a picket fence, as they did when the second owners, Augustus and Mary Crane, lived here. Crane also grew vegetables, fruits, and flowers with the aid of a full-time gardener, as well as keeping chickens and cows. His copy of *The Young Gardener's Assistant*, complete with his handwritten notations, was found in his library.

The newly redesigned herb garden incorporates a formal entrance with a brick path and a Victorian rose arbor. Today, the herbs found in the garden include bee balm, thyme, chives, purple basil, both curly and Italian parsley, yarrow, oregano, and lavender.

The full-sun garden features dazzling perennials and annuals, for Victorian gardeners loved bright colors. Its beds include primrose, forget-me-not, bleeding heart, columbine, peony, coralbells, red bee balm, double orange daylily, chrysanthemums, hardy ageratum, and daisies. Something is always in bloom from early spring through late fall, and the plantings are spectacular even on an overcast day.

Standing beside an informal English-style border planted with peonies and coralbells, an ornate gazebo is decorated with antique cast-iron bands of oak leaves and acorns rescued from a house in Morristown by the late Dorothy Harvey, who was instrumental in having Acorn Hall deeded to the Morris County Historical Society. From April through June, the garden is abloom with Korean azalea, Japanese weeping cherry, hundreds of white narcissus, Jacob's ladder, and Dutchman's-breeches, whose flower heads resemble white pantaloons hanging upside down. At the rear of the house you'll see semicircular beds of period roses; Peegee hydrangea, blue and white hydrangeas, peonies, and two handsome beech trees on your way back to the driveway.

NOTE: Inside Acorn Hall are many original furnishings, including a printed velvet rug in the formal parlor, trompe l'oeil effects decorating a bedroom set, Oriental porcelains, and numerous mid-Victorian items donated by local families, plus several "made-in-Morristown" pieces. The state's only Victorian research library is also housed here.

22
Macculloch Hall Gardens

LOCATION ❧ Morris County
45 Macculloch Avenue
Morristown 07960
973-538-2404

GARDEN SIZE ❧ Less than 1 acre

ADMISSION ❧ Fee

WHEN TO VISIT ❧ *Garden:* Dawn to dusk daily, year-round. *Museum:* Wednesday, Thursday, and Sunday 1–4, year-round; closed holidays. Group tours by appointment. The roses reach their peak in June.

HIGHLIGHTS ❧ Outstanding collection of old-fashioned roses; wisteria brought here by Commodore Matthew C. Perry; an adjacent historical museum housed in a grand, Federal-style mansion.

FACILITIES ❧ Rest room; handicapped-accessible

Come prepared to spend an entire morning or afternoon strolling through the garden either alone or on a guided tour, and leave time to explore the adjacent handsome, redbrick, Federal-style mansion, which was occupied by descendants of the Macculloch family for 139 years.

George Perot Macculloch, a Scotsman born in Bombay and educated in Edinburgh, built the house for his wife and two children in 1806. He was an adventurer, a scholar, and a dreamer, but he's remembered best as the planner and builder of the Morris Canal. A 102-mile waterway that ran from Phillipsburg on the Delaware River to Jersey City on the Hudson, it was acclaimed as one of the greatest engineering feats of the 19th century. It climbed and descended nearly 1,700 feet in elevation along its course; traversing it was made possible by a series of 23 inclined planes.

The mansion, now known as Macculloch Hall Historical Museum,

Lilies at Macculloch Hall Gardens

houses fine collections of 18th- and 19th-century English and American decorative arts, presidential china, and Oriental rugs. The Hajji Baba Club Library houses a wonderful collection of drawings and prints by cartoonist Thomas Nast, who lived opposite the Macculloch family. After the property was purchased by philanthropist and former Morristown mayor W. Parsons Todd, the gardens were restored and opened to the public as a memorial to the Macullochs and the mansion was opened in 1953 as a historical museum.

Planted for seasonal bloom and maintained by the Garden Club of

Morristown, the gardens are particularly outstanding in June, when the magnificent old-fashioned roses are in bloom. Among the beauties are 'Maiden's Blush Alba', the hybrid perpetual 'Ferdinand Picard', pink 'Grootendorst', the 'Old McHall' rose, the 'Seafoam' shrub rose, and floribunda 'Fragrant Delight'.

In addition to an outstanding rose arbor and attractive flower border lining the paths on this spacious lawn, there's a lovely old wisteria climbing up the back porch that was brought here from Japan by Commodore Matthew C. Perry. You won't have trouble identifying it, not only because of its magnificence, but also because masses of bees are attracted to its intensely fragrant, purple blossoms.

23
Frelinghuysen Arboretum

LOCATION ❧	Morris County
	53 East Hanover Avenue
	Morristown 07962
	973-326-7600
GARDEN SIZE ❧	127 acres
ADMISSION ❧	No charge
WHEN TO VISIT ❧	8 AM–dusk, year-round. Peak bloom for witch hazels and hollies is January, February and March; daffodils, cherries, magnolias, lilacs, rhododendrons, peonies, and dogwoods bloom in April and May; crab apples in May and autumn; azaleas in May to early July; roses in June and September; fall color peak is October.
HIGHLIGHTS ❧	Historic mansion; Braille trail, nature trail; specimen trees and numerous gardens on the grounds
FACILITIES ❧	Rest room, drinking water, gift shop, horticultural reference library; handicapped-accessible
EVENTS ❧	Summer gardening day camp; Harvest Show; lectures, concerts, classes, films, and more. Call for schedule.

Although officially known as an arboretum, where a collection of woody trees and shrubs have been cultivated for educational and scientific purposes, the Frelinghuysen Arboretum also features a number of small, beautiful gardens on its 127 lush acres.

An excellent place to begin is at the administration building, where descriptive folders and trail guides are available. The Blue Trail begins to the right of the front door, where dense beds of pachysandra boast white-spiked flowers in early May and are surrounded by huge rhododendrons.

Magnolias in bloom at Frelinghuysen Arboretum

Along the trail you'll see the Japanese pagoda tree, which bears white clusters of flowers in August; usually planted near Buddhist temples, it is also known as the "dirty" tree because it drops its fruits, flowers, and leaves on the ground. In the white oak woodland area you'll find dogwoods, azaleas, and tulip trees. Many of the specimen trees found on these grounds are taller than their predicted heights: the false cypress, a feathery evergreen native to Japan, is 76 feet high; a Norway spruce with pendulous, grace-ful branches is 88 feet tall. You'll also find a strikingly beautiful blue Atlas cedar and many specimen sugar maples, European lindens, black locust, ash, Eastern white pine, and red oak.

Two metal cranes grace the man-made pond in the Pikaart Garden, found along the Braille Nature Trail. Interestingly, the pond is filled not with water, but with bugleweed! In spring, when the bugleweed blooms, the bronze "water" turns a vibrant blue. Bog-type plants grow realisti-cally at the edge of the "pond," while primroses bloom in pink, red, and white. Native woodland shrubs, including andromeda, swamp hon-eysuckle, leucothoe, and mountain laurel, surround the site. Many plants in this area sport contrasting textures year-round, including dwarf horse-tail, a primitive spore-bearing plant related to ferns; kirengeshoma, a Japanese perennial with maplelike leaves and drooping yellow flowers; heart-leafed bergenia, with deep pink flowers in spring; and golden groundsel, which blazes gold in summer. Japanese water iris, greater wood rush, goatsbeard, astilbe, and black snakeroot make up the rest of the foliage.

The Mary Lindner Garden is filled with plants appropriate for rock and woodland gardens. Lindner, a member of Friends of the Freling-huysen Arboretum, nurtured the most difficult specimens in her home garden in Randolph Township; among the perennials she planted here are yarrow, mugwort, New England aster, buddleia (butterfly bush), Shasta daisy, pink and threadleaf coreopsis, border pinks, globe thistle, baby's breath, coralbells, blazing star, Oriental poppy, and lamb's ear.

The Vera M. Scherer Garden demonstrates special methods and equipment that make gardening accessible to the disabled. The raised-bed gardens are positioned to eliminate bending and stretching; they provide the options of standing to work, sitting along the edge, or in a wheelchair, while individual planters, window boxes, and hanging bas-kets are at accessible heights. Although the vegetable, herb, and flower beds have been designed for the disabled, there are good ideas here for every gardener.

The Beth Fisher Winter Garden was created to be enjoyed in all seasons—particularly winter, when the hawthorns, hollies, and skim-mias bear berries. The yellow-twig dogwood displays interesting gold-colored bark, and the hellebores, snowdrops, adonis, winter aconite, and winter jasmine all bear winter fruits. Uncommon evergreens in this garden include the feathery Chinese plum yew, the thick-needled Japanese umbrella pine, and the fragrant blooming sweet box. Daffodils bloom in spring, and summer features dead nettle and daylilies.

The Watnong Rock Garden features special plants and shrubs

that are perfect for small rocky areas, such as rock cress, heart-leaved bergenia, maiden pink, shooting star, Japanese shield fern, stonecrop sedum, bog rosemary, witch alder, and creeping wintergreen. The unique garden is dedicated to the memory of Don and Hazel Smith, who contributed greatly to the arboretum's collections of specimen conifers, flowering trees, and shrubs, particularly the collection of dwarf Hinoki cypress.

The Cottage Gardens are filled with old-fashioned flowers that casually spill over the walkways and create a kaleidoscope of color. This style of garden design is believed to have evolved during the 19th century, as flowers were increasingly added to practical kitchen gardens to add interest and beauty; by the end of the Victorian era, the style had become more formal. Here you'll find yarrow, sneezewort, blue star, dwarf goatsbeard, aster, clustered bellflower, purple and white coneflowers, cranesbill, daylilies, tree peony, phlox, primrose, and common thyme, among others.

In 1969, Matilda E. Frelinghuysen left the property to the Morris County Parks System for the enjoyment of the public. The administration building is housed in the Colonial Revival–style Whippany Farm mansion built as a summer home by her father, George, in 1891. There he ran the grounds as a farm, and provided fresh flowers and dairy products for the family's winter residence in New York City. The house, which is listed on the National Register of Historic Places, is most impressive inside as well as out.

24
Schuyler-Hamilton House Herb Garden

LOCATION ❧ Morris County
3 Olyphant Place
Morristown 07960
973-267-4039
GARDEN SIZE ❧ Pocket-sized
ADMISSION ❧ *Garden:* No charge. *House:* Fee.
WHEN TO VISIT ❧ *Garden:* Dawn to dusk daily, year-round. *House:* Tuesday and Sunday 2–5, and by appointment.
HIGHLIGHTS ❧ Medicinal herb garden; historic house
FACILITIES ❧ None

The garden where Dr. Jabez Campfield grew his marigolds, balsams, and medicinal herbs during the Revolutionary period is long gone. But thanks to the Home Garden Club of Morristown, a replica of his garden, now consisting of old-fashioned flowers and culinary and medicinal herbs, was planted in 1964. Because the Morristown chapter of the Daughters of the American Revolution (DAR) purchased and refurbished the house in 1923, visitors can now admire its lovely Colonial architecture, with features like hand-hewn oak beams, H and L hinges, and original chair rails.

Tiger lilies and annuals now brighten the side of the house each spring, while the garden, which includes a sundial, is reachable over an attractive brick walkway flanked by ivy, boxwood, rhododendron, and hosta. Although the garden is pocket-sized, it's worth a visit combined with a tour of the Schuyler-Hamilton House.

Dr. Campfield, an Army surgeon, owned this home when it was originally located on the King's Highway between General George Washington's headquarters and his camp. According to historians,

Washington and his troops camped in Morristown near Dr. Campfield's home during one of the coldest winters of the Revolutionary War. Washington and his aides stayed in the nearby home of Mrs. Theodosia Ford. When Dr. Campfield offered his home to the officers, Dr. John Cochran, a member of Washington's staff, accepted, bringing his wife, who was the only sister of General Philip Schuyler, with him.

Washington's aide Alexander Hamilton was supposedly swept off his feet when he was introduced to General Schuyler's daughter, Elizabeth, who was visiting her aunt, Mrs. Cochran. The Campfield house was already a favorite gathering place for young officers, and Hamilton showed up frequently to court Elizabeth, whom he called "my Betsy." People who knew him found it amazing that he could conduct vital and delicate war correspondence for General Washington and simultaneously court Betsy with ardent love letters. When the first spring flowers bloomed among Dr. Campfield's boxwood hedges, Hamilton announced his formal betrothal to her. The wedding was held in Albany the December of the same year, 1780.

After Dr. Campfield died in Morristown in 1821, the house passed into other hands. The new owners moved it a few hundred feet from its original position to its present location.

25

Shakespeare Garden at the College of St. Elizabeth

<table>
<tr><td>**LOCATION**</td><td>❧</td><td>Morris County
2 Convent Road
Convent Station 07961
973-290-4000</td></tr>
<tr><td>**GARDEN SIZE**</td><td>❧</td><td>Less than 1 acre</td></tr>
<tr><td>**ADMISSION**</td><td>❧</td><td>No charge</td></tr>
<tr><td>**WHEN TO VISIT**</td><td>❧</td><td>*Garden:* Dawn to dusk daily. *Greenhouse:* Hours vary.</td></tr>
<tr><td>**HIGHLIGHTS**</td><td>❧</td><td>Flowers and herbs mentioned in Shakespeare's plays and poems; greenhouse containing goldfish pond, succulent room filled with bromeliads, and tropical room with birds of paradise and a banana tree</td></tr>
<tr><td>**FACILITIES**</td><td>❧</td><td>None</td></tr>
<tr><td>**EVENTS**</td><td>❧</td><td>Plant sale in September</td></tr>
</table>

The idea for this unique garden, where each plot is devoted to the flowers mentioned by Shakespeare in his plays or poems, originated in 1920 after the College of St. Elizabeth was approached to contribute flowers for the renovation of Shakespeare's birthplace at Stratford-upon-Avon. Having accepted the invitation, Sister Helen Angela—the first Sister in the nation to receive a Ph.D., and a botany professor at the college from 1907 until her death in 1951—immediately began growing primroses, a flower treasured by the English. And primroses were among the first flowers she planted in the college's new Shakespeare Garden, which opened to the public in 1931. The garden is now tended almost single-handedly by Sister Agnes Vincent, who began taking care of it in the 1970s when the college suffered from cutbacks. What she's accomplished since then seems like a miracle.

Each plot at the Shakespeare Garden at the College of St. Elizabeth is devoted to the flowers mentioned in a particular work of The Bard's.

The Elizabethans used the trunks of oak trees as edging, so railroad ties—the closest substitute—have been used to separate the plots. The first plot, called The Taming of the Shrew, is filled with roses, pansies, and ivy, plus the Johnny-jump-up, the only pansy known in Shakespeare's time. A symbol of love at first sight, Elizabethans referred to it as Cupid's flower. The second plot, Much Ado About Nothing, contains wild or canker roses, referring to Don John's rebellious saying, "I'd rather be a canker in the hedge than a rose in his grace." Here, too, are plantings for Venus and Adonis: white and red roses, violets, primroses, anemones, and narcissus.

Nearby are plantings for *Othello*: poppy, mandrake, fig, and aconite. *Richard II* inspired the next plot, which is filled with marjoram, rue, violets, and balm, the emblem of anointment. The Twelfth Night features violets, flax, roses, and boxwood. If you recall the lines from *The Tempest*, "He was the ivy which hid my princely trunk," you'll know you're at the right place when you reach the ivy and tiger lilies.

Outside the conservatory are lush angel trumpet and morning glory vines; nearby are stands of thistle that attract flocks of goldfinches and butterflies. Inside thrives an amazing array of bromeliads, birds of paradise, night-blooming cereus, and banana trees—and a goldfish pond with quite a few frogs.

NOTE: Don't leave without strolling through the peaceful grounds and stopping in at the stone chapel, which was built in 1909 (entered through the main building). In 1850, wealthy families enrolled their daughters in high school here, and by 1899 the College of St. Elizabeth opened its doors. Today, 2,000 students attend the coed college for undergraduate, master's degree, weekend, and continuing education programs, but only women are allowed to live on campus.

26
Florence and Robert Zuck Arboretum

LOCATION	❧	Morris County
		Drew University
		Madison Avenue
		Madison 07940
		973-408-3358
GARDEN SIZE	❧	Approximately 3 acres
ADMISSION	❧	No charge
WHEN TO VISIT	❧	Dawn to dusk daily, year-round
HIGHLIGHTS	❧	Variety of native and introduced tree species; glacial ponds; and excellent bird-watching
FACILITIES	❧	Walking trail

The Florence and Robert Zuck Arboretum, used by the students and faculty of Drew University, serves as a living laboratory for students of botany and ecology.

Fortunately, visitors are also welcome to explore the attractive arboretum, which sits on Drew University's 186-acre wooded campus. Many of the plants you'll be admiring are a reminder of the beautiful gardens that existed on the estates that once occupied this land. Their plantings formed the nucleus of the collection. Recognizing its value as a natural laboratory for research and teaching, Drew University created the arboretum in 1980.

In spring, watch for kingfishers, wood ducks, green herons, great blue herons, pileated woodpeckers, red-bellied woodpeckers, and warblers, as well as many other small songbirds. During this time, wildflowers—purple myrtle, and the stunning pink and white spring beauty—decorate the forest floor.

The land you'll be walking on was formed when the last continental glacier passed through approximately 12,000 years ago. According to Dr. Sara Webb, chair of the biology department at Drew, "as the glacier receded and the chunks of ice it left behind melted, tiny dells were formed. About a century ago, people sealed and filled these depressions with water to form ponds. Two of them are still visible today. Long Pond, filled with plankton, painted turtles, and brown bullhead catfish, and Round Pond, home to carp, goldfish, and painted turtles, attract wildlife year round."

The major trees in the arboretum, including white oak, black oak, American beech, and sugar maple, are all native to the United States. The exception is the Norway maple, an introduced ornamental tree that is invading nature preserves.

The arboretum does not have labeled ornamental plantings because, notes Dr. Webb, "it is a garden that we are allowing nature to reclaim. Fallen trees are left to support mosses and fungi; the undergrowth is unmanicured and wild." To add to your enjoyment, bring along a tree identification book. Afterward, stroll the grounds, where you'll find a variety of specimens including dogwood, pin oak, black walnut, magnolia, wild black cherry, cypress, pine, white spruce, and Scotch pine.

27
Cora Hartshorn Arboretum

LOCATION ❧ Essex County
324 Forest Drive South
Short Hills 07078
973-379-3587
Web site: www.hartshornarboretum.com

GARDEN SIZE ❧ Approximately 16.5 acres

ADMISSION ❧ No charge

WHEN TO VISIT ❧ *Trails:* Dawn to dusk daily, year-round. *Nature Center:* Monday–Saturday 9–4:30 except when classes are held. Call first.

HIGHLIGHTS ❧ Arboretum, bird sanctuary, walking trails, nature center

FACILITIES ❧ Rest room and drinking water available when nature center is open.

EVENTS ❧ Guided trail walk on first Sunday in May; Open House and birdseed sale on second Saturday in October; maple tapping January and February; various activities year-round. Call for a free calendar of events.

Artist and naturalist Cora Hartshorn recorded 72 species of birds and dozens of varieties of wildflowers on these grounds, given to her by her father, Stewart Hartshorn, the founder of Short Hills. By 1938 she had created 3 miles of paths through the 16.5 acres of wild woodland overlying a series of small hills and valleys formed along the terminal moraine, a ridge composed of glacial rock fragments. Thanks to Ms. Hartshorn's generosity in bequeathing her Arboretum and Bird Sanctuary to Millburn Township in 1958, visitors can enjoy some of what she observed and cherished there.

The holly glows during freezing weather with its glossy evergreen leaves and the bright red berries borne on the female trees. The deciduous trees can be identified even in the winter by their silhouette and by the color and texture of their bark. The white oak is easy to identify by its thin, gray, scaly bark, while the dogwood hides its flowers and leaves in tiny reddish buds tucked neatly into forks and prongs. If you spot a few prickly balls clinging stubbornly from branches, you've found the sweetgum.

In spring there's color everywhere: in the lush stands of brilliant mountain laurel and rhododendron; in the shadbush, one of the earliest of the white-flowered shrubs to bloom; in the rust-tinged dogwood, a favorite among mockingbirds and catbirds; and in the over 80 species of wildflowers.

At the amphitheater where dance and music programs are held—a natural terminal moraine hole known as the Fawn Dell—there's an abundance of holly, shadbush, multiflora rose, highbush blueberry, azalea, and a variety of ferns. These fern species—the maidenhair, Christmas, cinnamon, interrupted, lady, and royal ferns—date back almost 300 million years.

On the way out, stop in at Stone House. The Nature Center features changing exhibits as well as a small collection of live animals, including a rabbit, ferret, garter snake, lizard, and cricket. The house, designed in 1931 by architect Bernardt E. Muller, is built of fieldstone and trap rock obtained from nearby quarries, with rafters made of hewn oak trees from Hartshorn land.

NOTE: South Mountain Reservation, a bit further north, has a picnic grove, sensational views, and hiking trails. Restaurants abound in the area.

28
Crane House Museum Gardens

LOCATION ❧ Essex County
110 Orange Road
Montclair 07042
973-744-1796

GARDEN SIZE ❧ 2 acres

ADMISSION ❧ No charge

WHEN TO VISIT ❧ *Garden:* Dawn to dusk daily, year-round. *House:* Wednesdays 1–4; Sundays 2–5.

HIGHLIGHTS ❧ Rose, herb, and fragrance gardens, historic Federal mansion

FACILITIES ❧ Rest room; partial wheelchair access; research library; country store

EVENTS ❧ Crane House tours held September through June; craft classes; old-fashioned holiday celebrations. Call for a schedule.

A visit to the Crane House Museum Gardens is an excellent way to experience the typical home garden of the 18th and 19th centuries.

From the moment you turn into the driveway flanked with massive rhododendrons, you'll no doubt feel that the gardens surrounding the Crane House are special. Built in 1796, the house—listed on the National Register of Historic Places—changed hands many times after Israel Crane, its original owner, died. Originally, it was located several blocks away, but in the early 1960s, when word got out that it was scheduled to be demolished, concerned citizens quickly formed the Montclair Historical Society in order to preserve the building. Successful, they moved it to this location in 1965.

Today, costumed docents demonstrate how Fanny Pierson Crane

The plots surrounding the Crane House replicate typical home gardens of yesteryear.

prepared meals for her husband, Israel, and their five children in rustic colonial fashion on an open hearth and beehive oven. While her husband's general store supplied a few of the necessary goods, Fanny grew almost everything else on the family's original 86-acre homestead. In addition to food, in her garden she grew the herbs for flavoring foods and beverages; for making toiletries, including colognes, shaving lotions and hair lotions; and for medicinal purposes.

According to docent Kathy Rafferty, Fanny always had a supply of herbal remedies known as "simples," on hand. These included feverfew, which she used for bringing down fevers; spearmint, pennyroyal, and parsley for treating biliousness; chamomile for consumption; and foxglove for pneumonia. She also made a product called Dine's Lady's Complexion Soap, named after the slave who took care of her housework.

A replica of Fanny's "pleasure" garden has been incorporated into the sloping lawn area. There, fruit trees such as the Baldwin apple, Seckel pear, and common plum border a footpath. The garden also features numerous flowering shrubs, including lilac, mock orange, viburnum, sweet-shrub, and old-fashioned roses, with 'Eglantine', 'Empress Josephine', and 'De Meaux' among them. Nearby is an attractive gazebo, similar to one Fanny most likely entertained friends in, where she'd serve tea made from the New Jersey tea shrub.

Since lawn mowers weren't invented yet, the Cranes used a flock of sheep, called croppers, to munch on the grass outside their back-door garden. The professionally designed garden beside the house today, typical of that period, contains rosemary, marjoram, tarragon, sage, parsley, thyme, chives, caraway, mints, basil, and savory, as well as rhubarb, strawberries, and currants.

Nathaniel Crane, Israel's relative, built his own modest home nearby in 1818, but it, too, was moved to these grounds (in 1974) and restored as a general store similar to the one Israel ran. It now houses a 19th-century post office and has gift items for purchase, including jams, jellies, potpourri, sachets, dried flower arrangements, toys, and crafts. Here, museum guides demonstrate how the candle merchants of that era made candles in quantity, how straw-type annuals and perennials were used for drying and crafts, and what life was like inside Israel's and Nathaniel's homes.

29
Van Vleck Gardens

LOCATION ❧ Essex County
21 Van Vleck Street
Montclair 07042
973-744-0837
GARDEN SIZE ❧ More than 5 acres
ADMISSION ❧ No charge
WHEN TO VISIT ❧ Daily, May through October, 1–5
HIGHLIGHTS ❧ Specimen wisteria and rhododendron
FACILITIES ❧ Rest room
EVENTS ❧ Spring plant sale, Mother's Day Reception;
Sunday-afternoon musicals in May. Call for a
schedule.

John Muir believed that "everybody needs beauty as well as bread, places to play in and pray in, where nature may heal and cheer and give strength to body and soul alike." The enchanting gardens surrounding the Van Vleck house—created over 80 years ago—would most likely meet with Muir's approval.

To begin your self-guided tour, pick up a map of the grounds on the rear terrace, where Chinese wisteria adorns the Courtyard Garden. Each May, these 60-year-old beauties display fragrant ten-inch lavender blossoms. There you'll also find a ground cover of periwinkle, and honeysuckle fills the air with its sweet perfume.

From the front of the terrace you'll have a sweeping view of the manicured lawn, which is divided into several sections planted with royal azalea, Kousa dogwood, bigleaf hydrangea, mountain laurel, Japanese andromeda, rhododendron, cedar of Lebanon, eastern red cedar, and highbush blueberries. Below the back terrace, you'll find three yellow rhododendrons, especially lovely in early June, that owner Howard Van Vleck hybridized and propagated. Named for the members of Van

Vleck's family, who lived here for over 50 years, the 'Howard Van Vleck', 'Betty Van Vleck', and 'Carolyn Van Vleck Pratt' rhododendrons have been registered with the Royal Horticulture Society.

Among the azaleas abloom along the Azalea Walk in spring, you'll see orange mollis, 'Coccinea speciosa', indica, white find, Blaauw's pink, Hershey's red, snow, coralbells, Stewartstonian, and pinshell. The nearby Rear Garden is filled with specimen trees and shrubs, including a majestic dawn redwood, blue Atlas cedar, Korean spice viburnum, saucer magnolia, star magnolia, Chinese holly, Scotch pine, and a multitude of rhododendron and azalea. The Carriage House Garden is home to another unusual collection, including Arizona cypress, the Japanese scholar tree, leatherleaf mahonia, Japanese euonymus, and yet more rhododendron and azalea that bloom in every imaginable color.

In Mother's Garden, near the upper lawn, you'll find mountain silverbell, slender deutzia, flowering dogwood, and Japanese wisteria. The Drying Yard, nearer to the house, is filled with white enkianthus and Japanese yew. Hundreds of bulbs make a showy appearance each spring: Camassia, a plant that provided a staple food for Native Americans, and Italian arum are just two. The greenhouse, built in the early 1920s, is where Howard Van Vleck spent much of his time grafting and cutting in order to propagate new varieties of plants. Today it's used by local school children, as well as to propagate plants for the property.

Joseph Van Vleck purchased the property in Montclair in 1870, and moved his family here permanently a few years later. His youngest son, Joseph Jr., an architect, designed and built the present U-shaped Mediterranean-style villa for his older brother, Will, in 1916. In 1939, Howard Van Vleck, one of Joseph Jr.'s sons, moved into it with his wife, Betty, and their children; they lived there for over 50 years. It was he who hybridized and propagated the rhododendrons on the back terrace. When Howard died in 1992, his children turned the property over to the Montclair Foundation, which proposed preserving the gardens and using the house and grounds for the benefit of the Montclair community and visitors. Howard Van Vleck's son, Roy, expressed his pleasure in knowing that this property will be permanently protected as "a place where people may continue to exercise the thoughtful, patient sensibilities of dedicated gardeners."

NOTE: Dogs, food, and drink are not allowed in the garden.

30
The Manor Gardens

LOCATION ❧ Essex County
111 Prospect Avenue
West Orange 07052
973-731-2360
GARDEN SIZE ❧ 22 acres
ADMISSION ❧ No charge
WHEN TO VISIT ❧ Dawn through dark daily, year-round; the gardens
are lighted at night
HIGHLIGHTS ❧ Elaborate formal gardens; gourmet restaurant
FACILITIES ❧ Benches; handicapped-accessible

Brides and grooms love it here. So do their wedding guests. In fact, so does everyone who comes to dine at The Manor, for it has consistently received awards as one of the best restaurants in the Garden State. But The Manor also cordially welcomes visitors who come not to dine but to stroll through its elaborate formal gardens, which Director of Facilities David Oster and his crew of 37 keep meticulously groomed year-round.

When Harry Knowles opened his three-room restaurant in 1956, the property consisted of cornfields, old gardens, and meadows. Since then he has transformed it into a fairy-tale garden; brick pathways lead to manicured lawns, formal annual and perennial beds, rose arbors, and a fanciful gazebo. Herb and vegetable gardens provide produce for the restaurant, and the fresh flowers on the tables are also grown on the grounds. They're all watered from three wells on the property that have been in operation since the turn of the century.

A boxwood-flanked brick path begins just outside the Terrace Lounge and leads past apple, pear, peach, and Japanese cherry trees that reach their peak in spring—the same time that over 15,000 tulips reach toward the sun in a riot of color. In early summer the daylilies and

The Manor Gardens

Japanese iris burst open, and the annual beds, filled with hundreds of begonias, petunias, and pansies, are at their best. To the right is a gazebo used by bridal parties, an arbor that's filled with white roses in June and July, and an 18th-century marble garden table and benches carved with ram's heads.

Several fountains are also featured, along with dogwoods, climbing vines, and rare shrubs. In autumn, chrysanthemums and hydrangeas are in perfect harmony against a backdrop of blue spruce, arborvitae, Japanese cedar, holly, and an understory of impatiens and dusty miller. The Starlight Garden features an ornate fountain, canna lilies, and tiered balconies, where dozens of huge urns brim with annuals and ivy. The garden is special even during winter, when hundreds of tiny Christmas lights twinkle against a backdrop of evergreens.

On your way back to the parking area, look for a variety of impatiens called 'Dapper Dan'; it's grown by a New Jersey nursery exclusively for The Manor.

31
Presby Memorial Iris Garden

LOCATION ❧ Essex County
474 Upper Mountain Avenue
Upper Montclair 07043
973-783-5974

GARDEN SIZE ❧ Approximately 2 acres

ADMISSION ❧ No charge

WHEN TO VISIT ❧ Dawn to dusk daily. Peak bloom is the last two weeks in May through early June.

HIGHLIGHTS ❧ Display of over 6,000 iris varieties including the fragrant blue-white 'Florentina', which dates from the 1500s, and 'Honorabile', a favorite 19th-century cultivar

FACILITIES ❧ Handicapped-accessible

EVENTS ❧ Annual Iris Festival. Call for date and time.

Hundreds of visitors from all over the world converge upon the Presby Memorial Iris Garden each year during the last two weeks in May and the first week in June, for that's when the tall bearded iris—the majority of the approximately 70,000 plantings—bursts into bloom. Now a National Historic Landmark, the gardens were laid out in 1927 by the Township of Montclair as a memorial to the late Frank H. Presby, nationally known horticulturist and founder of the American Iris Society. Now they are lovingly tended by the Montclair Garden Club and the Citizens' Committee of the Garden.

The iris gardens are in bloom from mid-May through October; the Dwarf and median irises peak around May 10; the Siberian, 'Louisiana', 'Spuria', and Japanese irises bloom from mid-June into July; and the taller "remontant" variety usually appears in late September through October.

The Presby Memorial Iris Garden is believed to be the largest of its type in the country.

Come during peak bloom in the spring, and you'll understand why this collection is believed to be the largest in the country.

Metal markers indicating the name of each variety, the year it was registered with the American Iris Society, and the name of the hybridizer, are in front of most plantings. In addition, you'll find the bearded 'Florentine' iris, which dates back to the 1500s, and native varieties that preceded it and have been invaluable in cross breeding. Look closely to see why the iris is called a trinitarian, meaning it has three of everything: three upper petals, or standards; three lower petals, or falls (which may be horizontal, known as flaring, or vertical, known as drooping); and three pollen-laden anthers protruding above three velvety beards. Naming and officially registering an iris is difficult, for consideration must be given to size, general shape, ruffling, fluting, lacing, standards, and fall, as well as to the sturdiness of the stem.

Admired the world over through the centuries for its beauty and curative powers, the iris symbolized communication. Iris, the goddess of the rainbow, transported messages of love from heaven to earth using a rainbow as a bridge. Tradition says that the iris was planted by Greek men on the graves of their beloved women as a tribute to the goddess; Egyptian Pharaoh Thutmose III had iris carvings added to his tomb 3,500 years ago; and Mohammedan soldiers carried iris rhizomes with them into battle to plant on the graves of their fallen warriors.

The iris has also been grown medicinally for a variety of uses. In both Elizabethan England and ancient China, the rhizomes were used to make face powder; European mothers made a pacifier of the chewy rhizome to soothe their cranky babies. Today, Mexico supplies France with tons of the plant's root for cosmetic manufacturing, and colored dyes are made from the blossoms and roots.

32
Avis Campbell Gardens

LOCATION ❧ Essex County
60 South Fullerton Avenue
Montclair 07042
973-746-9614

GARDEN SIZE ❧ Less than one acre

ADMISSION ❧ No charge

WHEN TO VISIT ❧ Dawn to dusk daily, early spring through mid-
September. Hours are subject to change, so call
ahead before visiting.

HIGHLIGHTS ❧ More than 275 varieties among 4,000 rose
bushes; Fragrance and Sensory Garden with
80 species of plants labeled in Braille; large
variety of perennials, herbs, and roses

FACILITIES ❧ Rest room when the building is open;
handicapped-accessible

EVENTS ❧ Private tours for groups on request; tours,
planting demonstrations, and cuttings available
Sundays in May from 2–4; members available for
gardening questions from April through early
November, 9–noon. Contact the Montclair
Garden Club at the above address.

A bronze plaque with the words COME REST A WHILE AND BROWSE IN THESE
GARDENS CREATED FOR ALL greets visitors to the Avis Campbell Gardens. And
rest you can, for this compact garden offers delightful sights and sounds.

For 26 years after its founding, members of the Garden Club of
Montclair searched for a permanent home in which to hold meetings
and to create a garden. In 1952, members were offered the facilities of
the Davela Mills Building for Social Agencies (now known as the United
Way building of the Essex Area). In exchange, it was agreed that club

The Avis Campbell Gardens are built in a wheel-of-life design.

members would look after the grounds and would create and maintain a garden adjacent to the building. Avis Campbell, a prominent professional landscape artist, designed the garden around a central fountain in a "wheel of life" design. In its new home, the club soon began to present free lectures and demonstrations on a variety of garden subjects.

No matter when you visit, you'll find dazzling displays. Early in spring, the large tulip plantings and flowering varieties of shrubs and trees put on a show. Later, annuals and perennials burst into bloom, among them are bleeding heart, foxglove, coralbells, poppies, peonies, columbine, and clematis. Summer brings alyssum, delphinium, phlox, day lilies, liatris, and astilbe, and fall is rich with asters and chrysanthemums.

Two garden areas are devoted solely to herbs, including wood sorrel, a tall, leafy plant sporting flowers during spring; sage, an aromatic beauty with lovely blue or lilac flowers; and rue, an evergreen perennial with a distinctive fragrance

During June and September, many varieties of roses, including 'King's Ransom', 'American Spirit', and 'White Delight', bloom in raised beds. Beds are surrounded by brick walkways, sedum abounds, and shocking pink and purple blossoms of clematis climb on trellises.

33
Brookdale Park Rose Garden

LOCATION ❧ Essex County
Grove and Montclair Streets
Bloomfield 07003
973-783-9595 or 973-482-7649

GARDEN SIZE ❧ Less than ¼ acre

ADMISSION ❧ No charge

WHEN TO VISIT ❧ Dawn to dusk daily during spring, summer, and fall.

HIGHLIGHTS ❧ Formal rose garden with over 1,200 rose bushes representing 140 varieties

FACILITIES ❧ Rest room; picnic area, playground; stocked lake for fishing, and hiking trails nearby in the 121-acre park

Designed by the landscape architects Frederick L. and John H. Olmsted, Brookdale Park encompasses 121 acres and includes 7 miles of walking trails, a lake for fishing, a picnic area, and a playground.

From May through September it is also home to Brookdale Park Rose Garden, a place to smell and photograph the blossoms of over 1,200 rose bushes of 140 varieties, spectacular against a background of huge evergreens.

The garden, created in 1959 with an original planting of 750 rose bushes that were donated by the North Jersey Rose Society, is maintained by the Essex County Parks Department. Each year, new varieties are added. Just a few of the beauties on display here include 'Touch of Class', 'Mr. Lincoln', 'Red Masterpiece', and 'New Beginning'. Here you'll also find a display of All-America Rose Selections; new hybrids are placed here for an entire season to allow home gardeners to see how they fare before being placed on the market.

34
United Nations Garden

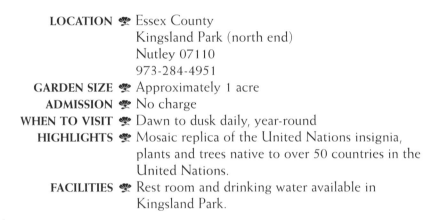

LOCATION ❧	Essex County
	Kingsland Park (north end)
	Nutley 07110
	973-284-4951
GARDEN SIZE ❧	Approximately 1 acre
ADMISSION ❧	No charge
WHEN TO VISIT ❧	Dawn to dusk daily, year-round
HIGHLIGHTS ❧	Mosaic replica of the United Nations insignia, plants and trees native to over 50 countries in the United Nations.
FACILITIES ❧	Rest room and drinking water available in Kingsland Park.

Implementing a new garden is not a project to be undertaken lightly; it requires dedication, careful planning, and lots of money. That's what the Home Garden Club of Nutley discovered when they decided to create the United Nations Garden, one of the first of its kind in the country. Many club members donated their time and effort make the garden a reality in 1961: Carl A. Orechio, then Commissioner of Parks and Public Property, found the beautiful 1-acre site on an island between branches of the Third River in Nutley's Kingsland Park; nurseryman Roy Blair designed the garden; and co-chairman Milton Anderson selected specimens. Memorial plaques were sold to raise money to purchase fill, topsoil, grass seed, trees, and shrubs, and the club accepted donations of plants as memorials to servicemen. Today the garden's plantings represent dozens of countries in the United Nations.

Norway spruce represents both Norway and Sweden; Austrian pine stands for Austria and Hungary; weeping willow for Jordan and Israel; azalea for Belgium; French lilac for France; littleleaf linden for Poland, the Czech Republic, and Slovakia; English hawthorn for Ireland; silver linden for Yugoslavia; thornless honey locust for Luxembourg; European ash for Denmark and Iceland; European hornbeam for Greece and Romania; white pine and shadbush for Canada; Russian olive for Russia and the Ukraine; and sacred Indian fir for Saudi Arabia, Yemen, and the United Arab Republic.

Two rose beds, including the 'Peace' and 'Girl Scout' varieties, represent the United Kingdom and were raised and contributed by Nutley's Girl Scout Troop 314. Plantings honoring the United States include the white pine, black alder, white dogwood, willow oak, and weigela. The Chinese plantings include a striking dawn redwood close to the river bank; two ginkgo trees, one of the oldest tree species on earth; and an Empress tree, which produces beautiful clusters of large, light violet flowers that appear before its large leaves appear.

When you reach the Japanese dwarf holly hedge, go through one of the cutout entrances that lead to an unusual 6-foot mosaic disk designed by Rolf Myller, one of six finalists in a nationwide contest for the Franklin D. Roosevelt Memorial in Washington, D.C. The mosaic, donated by the Nutley chapter of the American Association for the UN, is made of blue and white Venetian glass; the blue stones represent member countries in the UN.

After the garden opened, Anderson remarked, "We send one man to Congress or the United Nations Assembly to speak for thousands, but a tree planted in our United Nations Garden can represent millions." Most of all, Anderson hoped that visitors to the United Nations Garden would feel the same as poet Abbie Brown did when writing, "I lay at the foot of an ancient tree and let God's universe talk to me." I believe they will.

NOTE: Kingsland Park offers a vast lawn for ball tossing, picnicking, and watching the birds, plus a children's playground. Plan a visit to the Kingsland Manor Garden (see chapter 35, following); it's a 10-minute walk or 2-minute drive from the United Nations Garden.

35
Kingsland Manor Garden

LOCATION ❧ Essex County
Kingsland Street at Lakeside Drive
Nutley 07110
973-235-1974

GARDEN SIZE ❧ Less than ¼ acre

ADMISSION ❧ *Garden:* No charge. *House:* Fee.

WHEN TO VISIT ❧ *Garden:* Dawn to dusk. *House:* Call for hours.

HIGHLIGHTS ❧ Colonial-style garden; historic homestead

FACILITIES ❧ Rest room when house is open

EVENTS ❧ Christmas fair inside the house

When visitors arrive at Kingsland Manor, they automatically assume that the beautiful Colonial garden facing them is at the front of the house. I did—until I realized that the garden is actually situated at the rear of the house since the front entrance to Kingsland Manor was built overlooking the Third River. But no matter, for both the front (facing the river) and the back (facing the street) gardens are planted so attractively. After you're done exploring the relatively small gardens, don't miss taking a tour of the restored circa-1700s house.

Garden caretakers Ingrid and James Leonard note that spring ushers in crocuses, grape hyacinths, primroses, tulips, and daffodils in the back garden. The summer months bring delphiniums, with impressive tall spikes of bright flowers, and foxgloves, whose leaves produce digitalin, used for treating heart disease. Hollyhocks, in addition to being pretty to look at, have been used for centuries for food and as an insect repellent. Cosmos, a delicate annual with daisylike pink blossoms, attracts butterflies and hummingbirds; and an outstanding trumpet vine has delicately entwined itself around a lamppost. There are also bleeding hearts, rhododendrons, azaleas, alliums, pinks, cockscomb, scabiosas, hibiscus, and coleus, and in October, chrysanthemums.

Kingsland Manor Garden is adjacent to a house dating from the 1700s.

Among the shrubbery are two hollies and several hydrangeas, as well as ivies, ferns, a strawberry patch, and numerous herbs. Walking along the side of the house to the front garden, you'll see the gently flowing Third River and a small waterfall. If you have time, take a short stroll along the narrow dirt pathway near the water's edge to the United Nations Garden in Kingsland Park (see chapter 34).

Try to come when the manor house is open so you can see the property that Joseph Kingsland purchased for 11 pounds, 5 shillings in 1790 at a sheriff's sale after he had returned from Canada, where he had emigrated during the Revolution. It's estimated that the main section of the homestead was built around 1750 and the small summer kitchen annexed in the 1790s. The ballroom was added when Joseph Jr. inherited the homestead in 1860. The property changed hands many times until 1973, when a Nutley Planning Board member wisely petitioned the Town Commission to save the 1-acre site. The Commission then authorized the formation of the Historic Restoration Trust of Nutley, which turned Kingsland Manor into a landmark, museum, and resource for the community. Today the manor is a living history museum furnished with many period pieces dating from pre-1750 to the 1860s.

NOTE: Nearby Kingsland Park, where the United Nations Garden is located, has a vast lawn for ball tossing and picnicking, in addition to a children's playground.

36
Branch Brook Park

LOCATION ❀ Essex County
Mill Street entrance
Belleville 07109
973-268-3500

GARDEN SIZE ❀ Several acres of cherry trees within 486-acre
Branch Brook Park

ADMISSION ❀ No charge

WHEN TO VISIT ❀ Dawn to dusk daily, year-round; the cherry trees
bloom during the first three weeks of April.

HIGHLIGHTS ❀ The largest display of flowering cherry trees in
the world

FACILITIES ❀ Rest room, handicapped-accessible paths

EVENTS ❀ Cherry Blossom Festival in April. Call for exact
dates.

Most people travel to Washington, D.C., when the cherry blossoms burst into bloom. That's because they're not aware of one of New Jersey's best kept secrets—Branch Brook Park, home of the largest collection of flowering cherry trees in the world!

Listed on state and national registers of historic places, Branch Brook Park has the added distinction of being the nation's oldest and largest urban park, designed by Frederick Law Olmsted in 1895 as a place to promenade among formal gardens. Today, its 486 acres are enjoyed by residents of North Newark and Belleville for jogging, tennis, basketball, baseball, and bocci.

However, during the first three weeks of April, the northern end of the park attracts thousands of visitors who come to celebrate the annual Cherry Blossom Festival. The festival brings together people of many cultures to enjoy a traditional Japanese tea ceremony, Kabuki dancers, ancient Japanese court music, the art of origami, and a variety

Branch Brook Park is home to the world's largest collection of flowering cherry trees.

of crafts and foods sold by vendors.

Visitors also come to stroll along meandering paths to view vividly colored blossoms adorning more than 3,000 knarled trees of 28 varieties. The first 1,800 were given to the park in 1928 as a gift from philanthropist Caroline Bamberger Fuld in memory of her husband.

Among the beauties are single-flower varieties, such as the early flowering Higan cherry, identified by five petals and pink blossoms; the Sargent cherry, one of the largest of the flowering cherries sporting deep pink blossoms; the Yoshino cherry, with fragrant pale pink blossoms; and the weeping Higan cherry, with distinctive hanging branches and deep pink flowers. Among the semidouble varieties with six or more petals are the 'Autumnalis', which has a white, almond-scented flower; the 'Shirotae', with white blossoms, and the 'Amanogowa', a lovely tree with light pink blossoms. Among the double-flowering varieties are the 'Fugenzo', with reddish-pink blossoms early in the season, and the 'Shirofugen', which has large white blossoms that turn pink before they fade.

Cherry trees have been cultivated in Japan since the 7th century. Their blossoms are so revered there that for many centuries only the Japanese emperor and his court were allowed to view the blossoms, which have been portrayed in paintings and on pottery. Thankfully, today thousands can enjoy this outstanding display each year at Branch Brook Park.

37
Port Imperial Gardens

LOCATION ❦ Hudson County
Pershing Road at Port Imperial
Weehawken 07087
1-800-533-3779

GARDEN SIZE ❦ Approximately 1 acre

ADMISSION ❦ No charge except for parking

WHEN TO VISIT ❦ Dawn to dusk daily, year-round

HIGHLIGHTS ❦ Lush formal garden affording exquisite views of
Manhattan's skyline

FACILITIES ❦ Rest room in ferry terminal; benches;
handicapped-accessible

Long before passengers boarded the first ferry leaving Weehawken's Port Imperial for a 5-minute ride across the Hudson River into Manhattan, Arthur Imperatore, president of New York Waterway, knew that his ferry service would be a huge success. The journey by ferry not only helped ease traffic jams at tunnels and bridges, the short trip provided a pleasant, stress-free, scenic ride from the moment it was put into operation.

According to nurseryman Steve Cooper, Imperatore didn't stop with this successful venture. Instead, Cooper notes, he decided to create "a gardened portal to the city, one that would be a beautiful and functional waiting area for ferry customers." What Imperatore didn't foresee was that people would flock to this garden oasis just for the sheer pleasure of admiring the flowers while relaxing and enjoying a close-up view of the Manhattan skyline.

Construction on the garden, which Cooper designed, began in 1993. Multicolored brick paths that invite leisurely strolling divide the garden into eight symmetrical sections; a geometric tent stands at the center. Each section of the garden is bordered by a hedge of tightly knit green 'Fastigiata' hornbeams. Pruned to an even height, they give the illusion of individual rooms within the garden.

The east boundary is protected with silver lace vine along the bank, where there's a drop of approximately 10 feet at low tide. The formal section of the garden is bordered with Heritage birch, chosen for its lovely textured pink-and-white bark and for its hardiness. Beneath its airy canopy are plantings of Blue Girl and Blue Boy holly.

In the center of the garden stands a hornbeam, and two octagonal seating areas are ideal for relaxing and viewing both the colorful plantings and the skyline beyond. Each spring, over 1,500 mixed tulips are placed within the eight planting areas. Wisely, Cooper has varied the blooming time, height, and color to provide an ever-changing display, from the botanical tulips that bloom in April to the peony-flowered tulips that burst open in mid-May.

Over 400 sun-loving annuals can be found in each of the quadrant displays, including Elizabeth geraniums, Inca yellow marigolds, and prairie fire petunias. The perimeter beds, bordered by birch and holly, display taller annuals, such as blue salvia, brilliant hibiscus, and 15 different varieties of narcissus—a sight to behold in spring. After the first autumn frost, these annuals are replaced with Nagoya white and pink flowering kale for fall and winter color.

The walkway bordering the river leads past a long bed that is planted in a riot of colors. Cooper believes that this vibrant display—containing cleome, nicotiana, blue salvia, amaranthus, sunflowers, strawflowers, and statice—enhances the symmetry of the formal garden. Here, too, are numerous barrel planters displaying 18 varieties of hibiscus; they are outstanding from mid-May through September.

An allée of trellised tropical vines is planted each summer using mandevilla, honeysuckle, bower vine, and passion flowers. At the end of the summer, hanging baskets containing cascading ivy geraniums are hung from the arches, and by Christmas they're replaced with white pine roping, mixed greens, and lights.

Where do all these wonderful plants come from? The Imperatore Nurseries in New Hope, Pennsylvania!

NOTE: Take a picnic lunch to enjoy while watching the action on the Hudson River, or walk over to nearby Arthur's Landing Restaurant to see more dazzling plantings. The floor-to-ceiling wraparound windows in the restaurant afford a captivating view of Manhattan's skyline. You can also opt to take a round-trip ride on the ferry.

38

Durand-Hedden House
Herb Garden

LOCATION ❧ Essex County
523 Ridgewood Road
Maplewood 07040
973-763-0218

GARDEN SIZE ❧ ¼ acre

ADMISSION ❧ *Garden:* No charge. *House:* Donations appreciated.

WHEN TO VISIT ❧ *Garden:* Dawn to dusk daily. *House:* Open house
one day a month. Call for day and hours.

HIGHLIGHTS ❧ Traditional demonstration herb garden; 18th-
century farmhouse

FACILITIES ❧ Rest room when the house is open

EVENTS ❧ Annual Mother's Day herb and plant sale; Open
House once a month (call for hours); annual
regularly scheduled talks and events, including
Common Sense—a dried-flower-arrangement and
herbal-gardening demonstration; a garden party;
Muster Day; tours for school and Scout groups;
and workshops for adults in quilting, weaving,
and herb use. Write or call for a schedule

According to Joe Messing, chairman of the Maplewood Garden
Club, the Durand-Hedden House Herb Garden contains more plant
species than the herb garden at New York's Brooklyn Botanic Garden and
is recognized as one of the largest herb collections on the East Coast.

Spring is exceptional here, for that's when pink and red azalea,
orange-blossomed trumpet vine, forsythia, and hundreds of bulbs are in
bloom. A visual treat throughout the summer and fall, the garden wasn't
always this beautiful, notes Newt Meeker, Maplewood's Superintendent

of Parks and Shade Trees Department. "In fact, prior to 1980, this garden was nonexistent. When the Durand-Hedden House and surrounding land were purchased by the Township of Maplewood in 1978, the area this garden now occupies was only a lopsided hill." This quarter-acre demonstration herb garden was developed through the efforts of Meeker, the town, the Maplewood Garden Club, and the Durand-Hedden House Society.

Now maintained by the Maplewood Garden Club, the garden contains over 125 varieties of herbs, including approximately 12 basils; 10 sages; more than 15 mints; and *Lippia dulcis,* said to be ten times sweeter than sugar when its leaves are dried and crushed. You'll also find costmary, a biblical plant with large leaves that were often placed in bibles to give off a wonderful balsam fragrance when opened; sweet cicely, a perennial herb whose fernlike, pale-green leaves have a sugary taste; caraway, a biennial herb that's been used as a spice for over 5,000 years; bronze fennel, an attractive perennial valued as an herb, spice, and vegetable; and coriander, used in cuisines worldwide, with its attractive pink and white flowers.

Garden club members, who raise many of the annuals and tender perennials from seed, division, or cuttings, select about 40 varieties annually to manufacture numerous products that are sold at fund-raising events for the garden. The leaves of the chosen plants are then washed, dried, crushed, sieved, and made into various herb vinegars. One favorite, made of basil, oregano, savory, parsley, rosemary, tarragon, thyme, salad burnet, marjoram, and chives, is known as 10-herb vinegar. Lavender is used to make hair rinse, soap, and sachets; catnip is made into a toy sachet for cats; and savory is used as a flea repellent for dog's beds.

The trees surrounding the property provide a marvelous backdrop. Japanese holly forms a border on the eastern side of the garden, where there are also low junipers and bushy azaleas; while the southern side contains boxwood. Behind the garden is an impressive Atlantic white cedar and a stately black walnut.

When you're done touring the garden, check out the inside of the Durand-Hedden House, a historic and architectural landmark, for a glimpse of American history from Revolutionary times through the early 20th century. The original structure of the 18th-century homestead, where authentically costumed docents demonstrate open-hearth cooking on a beehive oven, belonged to Obadiah Hedden. The detailed story of how the land was acquired is very interesting, as you'll learn while touring the property.

39
Maplewood Memorial Park

LOCATION ❧ Essex County
Corner of Valley Street and Oakland Road
Maplewood 07040
973-763-4202

GARDEN SIZE ❧ 24 acres

ADMISSION ❧ No charge

WHEN TO VISIT ❧ Dawn to dusk daily, year-round

HIGHLIGHTS ❧ A large variety of domestic and imported tree species; annual and perennial plantings; lily pond

FACILITIES ❧ Playground, ball fields, benches

EVENTS ❧ Daylong July 4 celebration with evening fireworks.

During the late 19th century, parks were being built throughout the country, for it was believed that if one could internally conceptualize the innocent forms of nature, these forms would eventually mold and shape one's character. Frederick Law Olmsted, a pioneer in the park movement, was hired to create a showplace park in Maplewood. Before the project began, Percival Gallagher, one of Olmsted's partners, commented that "the park, by its central location and situation in the valley of the Second River, must reflect the ideals of the town and stand out as one of its most striking natural features." Additionally, he thought that this park should "provide facilities for games and other suitable outdoor recreation, while at the same time, preserving and enhancing the natural character of the ground and presenting altogether an attractive and ornamental park."

When Maplewood's Memorial Park was dedicated in 1928 it did, indeed, meet Gallagher's requirements. The original plan called for "facilities for a lake, wading pond, chairs and seats all around the area, a promenade, playground, open fields, groves, a hill for coasting in the winter, flower gardens, a ball field, and walkway of paths that circle the entire park which is lined by hundreds of trees for shade and seclusion from the street." All but the wading pool was incorporated; the lake is now a lily pond; and through the years a picnic area hidden in a grove of pine trees has been added. The only buildings in the park are the attractive Maplewood Memorial Library and the Civic House, while around the park's perimeter, hidden by trees, is the equally attractive Maplewood Municipal Building, Police and Fire Departments, and the railroad station.

Although the self-guided nature trail booklet prepared by Maplewood's Eagle Scouts is no longer handed out, you can photocopy it at the library if you wish. The Scouts also thoughtfully placed identification markers in front of each tree. The self-guiding walk begins in back of the library near the bicycle rack where, a few feet further, you'll find a crab apple tree with particularly lovely pink flowers during spring.

Hundreds of bulbs have also been planted throughout the park. Around the perimeter you'll find English yew, begonias, salvia, canna lilies, and more, all maintained by Newt Meeker, Supervisor of Maplewood's Parks and Shade Trees Department, and his crew. After walking through the park, you might want to stroll through Maplewood to see the wonders its flower-oriented residents have accomplished, evident in the abundance of beautiful lawns and flower beds. According to Meeker, this love for flowers is largely due to Richard Walter's influence. When Walter settled in Maplewood after emigrating from Germany, he set out to create a special spirit within the community. He believed that "people are never too old to plant something; that dilapidated housing is brought about by general neglect of properties; and that if one lot on a block isn't tended, a creeping blight results." Walter began planting shrubs and trees in Memorial Park as the former superintendent of parks; he also began teaching an adult education class for those interested in learning how to seed, plant, and landscape.

During World War II, Walter planted a victory garden outside the 116-by-26-foot greenhouse that was built and donated to the town by the members of the Maplewood Garden Club. By 1974, when the greenhouse proved so popular that it couldn't accommodate any more people, the Maplewood Garden Club raised funds to build another 40-by-60 foot greenhouse adjacent to the old one. Again, volunteers dug the foundation, moved dirt, and mixed cement, and the Parks Department assembled it.

Since Walter's death, the adult garden course has been taught by

Raymond Rowe, past president of the garden club and an expert in herbs and perennials. In order to reserve a greenhouse space from September through June, people line up hours before registration opens. A small fee is charged for bench spaces in order to pay for heating the greenhouse, and any extra costs are absorbed by the Parks Department.

NOTE: After strolling through the park, spend some at the Durand-Hedden House, a historic and architectural landmark, with one of the loveliest herb gardens in the state (see chapter 38).

40

Dr. William Robinson
Plantation Herb Garden

LOCATION ❧	Union County
	593 Madison Hill Road
	Clark 07066
	732-381-3081
GARDEN SIZE ❧	1 acre
ADMISSION ❧	No charge
WHEN TO VISIT ❧	*Garden:* Dawn to dusk, daily. *House:* April through December on the first Sunday of the month, 1–4 PM.
HIGHLIGHTS ❧	Typical 17th-century herb garden; 1690 house listed on the state and national registers of historic places
FACILITIES ❧	Rest room and water when the house is open
EVENTS ❧	Colonial Game Day; Garden Harvest. Call for a schedule.

"During the 17th century, it was common for families to plant an herb garden outside the kitchen door," notes Connie Brewer, historian at the Dr. William Robinson Plantation House. "Herbs were grown to add zest to foods, used for beauty aids, and as fragrance to cover up unpleasant odors in the home. Since in those days people didn't rely on the medicine cabinet, they looked for cures in their gardens." In the Rahway, New Jersey, vicinity, many relied on Dr. William Robinson, a physician and surgeon who moved there from Scotland in 1690. In his kitchen garden, Dr. Robinson planted numerous medicinal herbs that would be useful in treating his patients' various ills.

Although the garden here today was planted in 1977, it contains many of the same herbs Dr. Robinson used. Majestic century-old maples stand guard over it, and among the plantings are furry lamb's ear, used as a bandage; lavender, used for treating muscular pain, headache, and giddiness; lemon balm, made into a tea to calm nerves and headaches; lovage, for treating liver and kidney ailments; mint, for stomach upset; agrimony, for curing colds, cuts, earache, and hemorrhoids; and comfrey, a favorite for bruises, coughs, and cuts.

Docents are dressed in period farm attire and antique farm implements are scattered around the perimeter of the garden. It's easy to feel drawn back to another era, especially if you explore the inside of this incredible farmhouse—now registered as a historic site—that was built for Dr. Robinson and his family in 1690. The foundation was excavated by hand, its fieldstone and boulder base held together with clamshell mortar, and the timbers and boards were hand-cut and planed by carpenters and joiners.

In addition to this land, Dr. Robinson owned hundreds of acres both in this area and in Monmouth County. Since large land holdings were often referred to as plantations in early Colonial days, when the property was leased to the Clark Historic Society for restoration and operation, with the provision that it be restored to its 1690 appearance and opened as a free museum, it was named the Dr. William Robinson Plantation.

Besides farming the land and practicing medicine in this house, Dr. Robinson later won fame as having performed the first autopsy (or dissection, as it was then referred to) for anatomical study in New Jersey.

Today, all three levels of the house—one of the few examples of 17th-century architecture in the nation with many features of the Tudor period—are open to visitors. The exterior has an unusual steep roof and small, diamond-paned casement windows. Inside there is a medicine room on the first floor, and a winding staircase leads to the chamber on the second floor. A cobblestone ramp leads down to the cellar, which served as a barn entry so that livestock could be stabled inside.

Among the many unique features discovered in this house are handhewn sills, beams, and gunstock posts with chamfered edges that have decoratively carved lamb's tongue and diamond endings. One of the highlights is the huge chestnut summer beam and cross supporting beams. All joining was done with mortis and tenon and dovetail joints that were pegged instead of being secured with nails and spikes. This method, called post-and-beam construction, was used until the mid-1800s.

41
Reeves-Reed Arboretum

LOCATION ❧ Union County
165 Hobart Avenue (near Route 24)
Summit 07901
908-273-8787

GARDEN SIZE ❧ 12½ acres

ADMISSION ❧ No charge

WHEN TO VISIT ❧ *Arboretum grounds:* Dawn to dusk daily, year-round. *House and office:* Monday, Tuesday, Thursday, and Friday, 9–3. There is a spectacular daffodil display in early April; the rose garden is at its peak in June.

HIGHLIGHTS ❧ Geological formations; rose and azalea gardens; wildlife habitat garden; perennial border; magnificent tree collection; botanical and horticultural library

FACILITIES ❧ Education Center; library; self-guided nature trail; rest room (open during office hours); gift shop

EVENTS ❧ Year-round events and programs for adults and children, including Rose Day in June; garden tour during spring; children's summer programs; Family Harvest Festival and bird seed sale in fall; December Holiday House Tour. Call for complete program schedule.

The Reeves-Reed Arboretum may be one of the state's best-kept secrets. Comprising 12½ acres of open fields, lawns, formal gardens, and natural hardwood forest, this lush oasis in the cosmopolitan town of Summit is within a stone's throw of Manhattan. In addition, it offers an unusual opportunity to see the geological formations known as "kettles." These depressions in the ground are believed to have formed when

Reeves-Reed Arboretum is an oasis filled with shrubs, wildflowers, ferns, roses, and trees.

chunks of the Wisconsin Glacier broke free approximately 10,000 years ago, lodged deep in the ground, and eventually melted.

The grounds, originally part of a Revolutionary War–era farm, were purchased by John H. Wisner in the late 19th century. After building an impressive Colonial Revival–style mansion, Wisner planted hundreds of daffodils. In 1916 he sold the property to Richard E. Reeves, who laid out gardens based on plans drawn by Calvert Vaux, a partner of Frederick Law Olmsted and a prominent New York landscape architect. Reeves also filled a kettle depression in front of the mansion with more daffodils—thousands to be exact (a similar kettle can also be seen along the East Trail in the wooded area). An herb garden and woodland trails were added after Charles L. Reed Jr. bought the property in the 1960s. In 1974, private citizens and town officials raised funds to establish the arboretum, which is now maintained through memberships, contributions, and the work of volunteers.

The grounds contain numerous shrubs, wildflowers, huge collections of ferns, herbs, roses, and a variety of native and imported trees. Check out the huge trees in the parking lot; the black and white oaks here are typical of the trees that were sent from America to England to supply the shipbuilding industry in the 1700s. An impressive Atlas cedar—a fragrant evergreen native to the Atlas Mountains in Algeria—stands at the corner of the mansion. Nearby stands a Canadian hemlock, the easiest of all the evergreens to identify by its needles, which are dark green on the upper side and silvery on the lower side. Near the Colorado blue spruce is a showy saucer magnolia, easily identified in winter by its fuzzy, insulating buds, and in spring by its large, saucer-shaped flowers that appear just before the leaves form. When you see a tree sporting wrinkled and silvery bark, you'll immediately know why the European beech is nicknamed the elephant tree. Once a favorite food among early settlers, its three-sided beechnut is a favorite food of squirrels and chipmunks.

A tall tulip tree stands majestically in one of the kettle holes; if you're here during the summer, look up to see the beautiful tulip-shaped flowers. In this area you'll also find dozens of perennial beds, tucked into nooks along a rock wall, that stay aglow through fall. The Fern Walk is delightful, and nearby are stands of mountain laurel and rhododendron, all spectacular during spring.

The Rose Garden reaches its peak during mid-June, when visitors can enjoy the beauty of a formal garden while learning about rose selection and care. Many of the rare and unusual species in this garden put on another show in September, along with colorful asters, chrysanthemums, and sedums. The last of the chrysanthemums peek out amid the autumn foliage in late October; winter is the time to appreciate the contrast of lovely red holly berries against a white blanket of snow.

NOTE: When the mansion is open, request a trail booklet and take the suggested self-guided walk through the grounds. Plan on spending a couple of hours walking leisurely—longer if you have a tree, bird, or wildflower identification book. Don't miss the gift shop; it's filled with unusual garden items.

42
Alice Ransom Dreyfuss Memorial Garden

LOCATION ❧ Essex County
Newark Museum
49 Washington Street
Newark 07101
973-596-6550

GARDEN SIZE ❧ 1 acre

ADMISSION ❧ *Garden:* No charge; donations accepted.
Planetarium: Fee. *Museum:* Parking fee.

WHEN TO VISIT ❧ Wednesday through Sunday noon–5; closed
Monday and Tuesday. Closed January 1, July 4,
Thanksgiving Day, and December 25.

HIGHLIGHTS ❧ Century-old trees, including an exceptional
copper beech; unusual sculpture

FACILITIES ❧ Handicapped-accessible; café; rest room; museum
shop

EVENTS ❧ Concerts in the garden; ongoing exhibitions
inside the museum. Call for a schedule

The moment you enter this garden, you'll leave all traces of busy
downtown Newark behind. Scattered around the perimeter of the vast,
well-manicured lawn is a huge variety of specimen trees over a century
old and a collection of sculpture dating from the 1960s and 1970s.

The Japanese dogwood growing next to the garden entry is particularly outstanding in spring when its showy, creamy flowers appear.
Nearby, to the left, spreading its strong limbs is a horse chestnut, named
for the huge, spiny fruit it produces, and a Kentucky coffee tree, recognized by its ovate leaflets, scaly, dark brown bark, and whitish, fragrant
flowers that appear from late spring through early summer. This coffee

Unique sculpture adorns the Alice Ransom Dreyfuss Memorial Garden.

tree provided beans for the troops stationed here during the Civil War.

Farther along on the left side of the path is a tall, beautifully shaped linden. Also known as basswood, this tree produces heart-shaped, sharp-toothed leaves. When laden with abundant clusters of fragrant tiny, cream-colored flowers in late spring or early summer, the tree is abuzz with honeybees.

In 1797, George Washington is reputed to have stopped to talk to students in the circa-1784 one-room schoolhouse. Sited beneath the shade of a white ash tree, the schoolhouse is flanked by a hickory and an ailanthus. During spring, the Japanese cherry, magnolia, and crab apple at this end of the garden put on a fabulous show. Following the path as it circles to the right, you'll come to a lovely group of trees, including a tall tulip that seems to reach to the sky; a red maple, boasting scarlet leaves in the fall; a pin oak with droopy bottom branches; a Norway maple; and a purple giant filbert.

Upon your return to the entrance you'll pass a 'Kwanzan' cherry that's dwarfed by one of the most magnificent and impressive copper beech trees for miles around. Tall and handsome, the beech provides welcome shade on a hot day; thoughtfully, benches have been placed beneath it. The wood of this tree is prized for furniture, tool handles, bowls, and much more. During winter, when the long, thin, sharp-pointed buds are obvious, Thoreau's words, "the spearheads of Spring," come to mind. Throughout the garden, there are attractive plantings of annuals and perennials.

Works of famous sculptors, including Grace Knowlton, Joel Perlman, David Smith, and Marjorie Strider, can be found in this delightful garden. One of my favorites is George Segal's whimsical *Toll Booth Collector*. Segal obtained a toll booth from the Holland Tunnel, coated it in bronze, and made a casting of Samuel C. Miller, director of the museum, holding out his hand to collect tolls.

NOTE: Guarded parking, adjacent to the museum and garden, is safe and inexpensive. If the weather cooperates, take a picnic lunch along to enjoy in the garden or try the delightful museum café. Afterward, spend the rest of the day exploring the outstanding collections inside the museum. They include one of the foremost collections of American art from the 18th through the 20th centuries; the Decorative Arts Collection with holdings of glass, ceramics, and textiles from the Renaissance to the present; permanent galleries with art from Africa, the Americas, the Pacific, and Asia; and the Ballantine House, a former 1885 beer-baron's mansion with a nationally recognized collection of approximately 15,000 decorative arts objects. Planetarium shows are held here on weekends, or you can join a gallery tour, offered daily.

43
Leonard J. Buck Garden

LOCATION ❧ Somerset County
11 Layton Road (off Route 202)
Far Hills 07931
908-234-2677

GARDEN SIZE ❧ Several acres

ADMISSION ❧ Donation requested

WHEN TO VISIT ❧ *Garden and Visitors Center:* Monday through Friday
10–4; Saturday 10–5; Sunday, noon–5. Closed for
major holidays and weekends in December,
January, and February.

HIGHLIGHTS ❧ Native and imported plants; a variety of trees,
including large dawn redwoods from China; rock
outcroppings; fern collection; ponds, meadow,
bird-watching.

FACILITIES ❧ Rest room and drinking water available when
visitor center is open; reference library.

EVENTS ❧ Plant sale in April

The late Leonard J. Buck believed that a garden should be "ecologi-cally correct and visually appealing . . . a place where one area moves naturally into the next, making it as pleasant to walk through as to sit in." After purchasing 33 acres of land in the 1930s, upon which he found evidence of the natural rock platforms and unusual outcroppings formed by the Wisconsin Glacier thousands of years earlier, Buck attempted to create such a garden, a quest that would ultimately span 40 years. Buck's garden not only gained recognition among private horticultural groups and professionals, it earned him the Gold Medal of the National Association of Gardeners in 1950, and is now recognized as one of the premier rock gardens in the eastern United States.

Buck worked with Swiss-born landscape architect Zenon Schreiber to preserve the natural look of the site; this meant retaining the original rock outcroppings as well as the native oak, beech, spruce, and locust trees. As they uncovered rock outcroppings they named and developed them; they include Little Rock, Big Rock, Horseshoe, Ivy, and Fern. To preserve the natural form of the rock, the only modifications they made were to create pockets and beds to accommodate the rare and common plants that Buck had collected from many corners of the globe.

If the visitors center is open, request a map; if not, most plants are tagged. The garden is fascinating year-round; rare and exotic rock garden plants are tucked in hundreds of nooks, and the wooded trails connecting the outcroppings are lined with wildflowers during spring. The yellow bells of the Canada lily appear among the swamp grasses in late spring; hundreds of primroses burst into bloom in May; June brings the lemony fragrance of sweet bay; and the red spires of the native cardinal flower attract both hummingbirds and visitors in late summer. Maidenhair fern thrives during the heat of the summer, while the red maples put on a glorious show in autumn.

One of the highlights of the garden is the F. Gordon Foster Hardy Fern Collection, which was donated by a Sparta resident in 1986. Among the collection are ostrich fern, cinnamon fern, and royal fern. Farther up the sloping path are giant shield ferns capable of exceeding 5 feet in height, as well as Christmas ferns, which remain green year-round.

Be sure to visit the flat, grassy promontory known as Big Rock, reachable from the entrance path. Rising about 20 feet above the lower meadow and pond, this ledge is filled with wildflowers, which grow freely from every crack. Ivy Rock, up the same slope, is a basalt formation fractured into vertical columns—an indication that it is close to the top of a former lava flow. Farther down the path is Reno Rock, which was supposedly named after Mrs. Buck threatened to divorce her husband if he didn't stop blasting the rocks with dynamite. Don't miss Azalea Field, where you'll find monkshood, joe-pye weed, bugbane, Japanese windflower, and rubrum lily from spring through summer.

Meandering walkways and wooded paths throughout the property lead past ponds, creeks, and meadows. Even the winter months are interesting; that's when some of the heathers are still in bloom, the fruits of the winterberry are bright red, and warblers, ruffed grouse, scarlet tanagers, sparrows, finches, and pileated woodpeckers are in evidence among the bare trees.

Through the years, famous botanists and horticulturists were invited to view Buck's special garden, which he had named Allwood. When Buck died in 1974, his wife, Helen, renamed the garden in his honor. In 1976, she donated it to the Somerset County Park Commission for all to enjoy.

44
Hunterdon County Arboretum

LOCATION ❧ Hunterdon County
1020 Route 31
Lebanon 08833
908-782-1158

GARDEN SIZE ❧ 73 acres

ADMISSION ❧ No charge

WHEN TO VISIT ❧ *Arboretum:* 8 AM–dusk. *Park Office:* Monday through Friday, 8–4:30; Saturday, 8:30–noon and 1–4:30; closed Sunday and holidays.

HIGHLIGHTS ❧ Distinctive trees and shrubs; native and exotic plants; greenhouse; children's garden; herb garden; two gazebos, including one built in 1893 that's believed to be the oldest in the state; hiking trails

FACILITIES ❧ Administrative headquarters of the Hunterdon County Park System; rest room and water when office is open. The front of the building and the trail leading to the gardens and gazebo is handicapped-accessible.

EVENTS ❧ Numerous workshops are offered year-round; topics include garden design, pruning, pest problems, and photography. Concerts and organized hikes are also held year-round. Write or call for a free calendar of events.

This 73-acre site was once the site of the largest known private nursery in the state. Today, according to chief naturalist Don Freiday, "it is a place where visitors can observe and study diverse plant life and many

The circa 1893 gazebo at the Hunterdon County Arboretum is believed to be the oldest of its kind in the state.

species of wildlife while walking through fields, pond, wetland, evergreen and deciduous forest habitats." The Furnas section supports an additional 32 acres of mixed hardwoods.

After parking, walk over to the Hunterdon County Park System's administrative building, where maps and rest rooms are available. The front walkway is lined with annuals, and the adjacent greenhouse is filled with house and garden plants grown on-site and used for demonstration purposes.

The trail outside the administration building leads to a formal garden that's been fenced in since 1997 in an attempt to keep the abundant deer population from destroying the plants. Nearby, to the right of the trail, are cool- and warm-season grasses. Squirreltail grass grows rapidly in March and April, producing flowers by the end of May, while the warm-season maiden grass grows quickly during July and August and produces seed toward the end of the summer.

The Arch Bed along the path to the gazebo is filled with a dazzling display of annuals and perennials. Here you'll also find a beautiful Katsura tree, identified by its tiny flowers in spring and its yellow, pink, and purple autumn foliage. The beautiful two-story gazebo was built in 1893 and moved here in 1978 from the Deats estate in Readington Township; it is believed to be the oldest of its kind in the state. Ranger Doug Kiovsky restored the gazebo with cedar support sections in 1997 and added the ornamental carvings of a sunburst, evergreen trees, and acorns.

Near the gazebo you'll find an All-American Selections Display Garden, planted with zinnia, petunia, celosia, salvia, and rudbeckia. Nearby is the Bouquet Garden, adorned with Italian white sunflower, salvia, cosmos, portulaca, lobelia, zinnia, miniature gladiolus, tiger lilies, and pompon dahlias. The small butterfly garden is planted with zinnia, echinacea, astilbe, and red salvia; the Memorial Garden features brightly colored daylilies, asters, 'Russell' lupines, and 'Autumn Joy' sedum. Toward the back gate, you'll find a wonderful assortment of herbs, including thyme, mint, basil, and lamb's ear.

A boardwalk erected by an Eagle Scout in 1988 meanders through the wetland area, where weeping willows can be found at one end and skunk cabbage, an early spring bloomer, at the other. There are also dozens of cattails, used by the animals for food and cover. Long ago, the downy seeds were used for stuffing in quilts and pillows, the seed heads as torches, and the young shoots eaten like asparagus.

A lone maple is on the right side of the Memorial Trail, while on the Two-line Trail—named for the northern two-lined salamander you might find here in warm wet weather—are massive grapevines that cling onto the trees with their long tendrils. Amur cork trees from Madagascar can be found on the left side of this trail. If you squeeze their soft and squishy bark, you'll know why it was used to make corks. The open area along the trail has been taken over by multiflora rose bushes that are quite thorny, but the rose hips produced on these shrubs during fall and winter attract lots of birds.

45
Cannonball Museum Gardens

LOCATION ❧	Union County
	1840 Front Street
	Scotch Plains 07076
	908-322-6700
GARDEN SIZE ❧	Less than ⅛ acre
ADMISSION ❧	*Gardens:* No charge. *House:* Fee.
WHEN TO VISIT ❧	*Garden:* Dawn to dusk daily. *House:* The first Sunday of the month and on special holidays, 2–4. Tours by appointment.
HIGHLIGHTS ❧	Geometrically designed flower and herb gardens and the Cannonball House Museum
EVENTS ❧	Garden weddings and house tours by appointment

As its bicentennial project, the Plainfield Garden Club designed and landscaped a beautiful geometric garden next to the historic Osborn Cannonball House—a Colonial saltbox-style white clapboard dwelling measuring only 33 by 29 feet. The original owners, Jonathan and Abagail Osborn, raised eight children here, three of whom enlisted in the local militia when the Revolutionary War broke out. Both British and Continental troops marched past this house, which was nicknamed the Cannonball House after a Colonial artillery man missed his target and accidentally fired a cannonball smack through a side wall.

The house is now carefully restored and furnished by the Historical Society of Scotch Plains and Fanwood. Visitors are invited inside to view the original wide floorboards, hand-hewn ceiling beams, beehive oven, recessed porch, wooden peg construction, wall plaster made of crushed oyster shells strengthened with animal hair, and the low ceilings and doors common to that period.

Although tiny, the gardens surrounding the house are quite striking and beautifully cared for by volunteers. They're also a fine example of what can be accomplished with a small plot. Stroll the handsome brick and wood chip paths leading into the geometric six-sided center plot filled with boxwood, yew, and geraniums with dazzling groupings of impatiens and low boxwood at the borders. A fenced-in area contains parsley, savory, and other herbs.

A second memorial garden given to the residents of Scotch Plains by the Loizeaux family in honor of Marion Foster Loizeaux, a member of the Plainfield Garden Club, contains numerous plants typical of those used in Colonial times. Here you'll find lavender, valued for its marvelous fragrance and often used in sachets or bath water; and hyssop, a compact, aromatic perennial in the mint family that's mentioned in the Bible. The huge, concave rock that adorns the center of this garden came from a home in Scotch Plains. According to historian Mrs. William Elliott, it was partially buried so that it served as a feeding trough for chickens.

Behind the house is an impressive grape arbor and an old-time privy. A variety of trees adorn the grounds, including holly, dogwood, and flowering crab apple, and benches have been thoughtfully placed to allow visitors to rest and absorb the beauty.

46

Shakespeare Garden at Cedar Brook Park

LOCATION ❧ Union County
Park Avenue
Plainfield 07060
908-527-4900

GARDEN SIZE ❧ Less than ¼ acre

ADMISSION ❧ No charge

WHEN TO VISIT ❧ Dawn to dusk daily

HIGHLIGHTS ❧ Numerous plants mentioned in Shakespeare's
works are on display.

FACILITIES ❧ Rest room

Cedar Brook Park, opened for public use in 1925, sits on 75 acres of former swampland and is named for a brook that runs through the property. The park also contains a small pond that's favored by children who come to fish for bass, bluegill, sunfish, and catfish.

A paved walkway leads to the Shakespeare Garden which, developed with the cooperation of the Plainfield Garden Club and the Shakespeare Society, was dedicated in 1927 on the 363rd anniversary of Shakespeare's birth. Today it's maintained by the Union County Park Commission and the Plainfield Garden Club.

While listening to the sound of honking Canada geese and mallards, you'll see approximately 40 plants that have been mentioned in Shakespeare's plays and sonnets. Plantings, including primroses, pansies, violets, narcissus, balms, and hollies, are arranged in geometrically designed flower beds and borders. Shakespeare was particularly fond of the pansy: he wrote in *A Midsummer Night's Dream*, "The juice of it, on sleeping eye-lids laid, / Will make a man or woman madly dote / Upon the next live creature that it sees."

Something is always in bloom from spring through fall, but summer is best: That's when the daylilies are in bloom and the bright red blossoms of the trumpet vine attract hummingbirds and butterflies. The garden also contains dusty miller, sedum, ivy, and holly, as well as spruce trees.

NOTE: During spring, more than 200 dogwood trees in over 60 varieties put on a spectacular display in the nearby arboretum.

47

Warinanco Park Gardens

LOCATION ❧ Union County
Warinanco Park
Off St. George Avenue (Route 27)
Roselle 07203
908-527-4900

GARDEN SIZE ❧ *Chatfield Memorial Garden*: 1 acre; *Azalea Garden*: 2 acres.

ADMISSION ❧ No charge

WHEN TO VISIT ❧ Dawn to dusk daily, year-round. Peak bloom for cherry trees, tulips, and azaleas is April and May; for annuals, June through September.

FACILITIES ❧ Rest rooms; fitness trail, playground, athletic fields, cross-country ski trails, ice skating rink, and paddle boats are located within the park

Ted Edzek, horticulturist for the Union County Parks System, calls the gardens at Warinanco Park "the county's prize jewels." They're especially beautiful in early April when the Japanese cherry trees and magnolias scattered throughout the 206-acre park put on a dazzling show. Later in the month, in the Henry S. Chatfield Memorial Garden—a formal garden established in 1936 and named in honor of the first president of the Union County Park Commission—over 14,000 Darwin tulips burst open in every color of the rainbow.

Although budget cuts have greatly diminished the size of Union County's gardening crew over the years, much effort has been put into maintaining both the 1-acre Chatfield Memorial Garden and the 2-acre Azalea Garden located just north of the Administration Building. The Azalea Garden, designed by Frederick Law Olmsted Jr. in 1936, was dedicated in 1957 in memory of the late Caxton Brown of Summit, one of the original park commissioners. According to Edzek, from an original planting of 26 species, the Azalea Garden has grown to include over 45 species, including native and exotic varieties and hybrids. The blossoms open in May in colors ranging from white, light pink, and deep red, to yellow, orange, and purple. If you can't visit the gardens until summer, don't worry: there will still be lots of color. Thousands of annuals, including dusty millers, impatiens, and marigolds, are planted in the Chatfield Memorial Garden once the tulips are gone.

Designed as a 206-acre city park close to transportation and within walking distance to many area residents, Warinanco Park, which is located in the towns of Roselle and Elizabeth, offers visitors many activities in addition to flower gazing, such as bicycling, basketball, ice skating in a closed rink, fishing, and boating.

NOTE: Picnicking is encouraged, as is walking on the grass.

Central
New Jersey

Duke Gardens

LOCATION ❧	Somerset County
	Route 206 (1.25 miles south of the Somerset
	Shopping Center)
	Somerville 08876
	908-722-3700
GARDEN SIZE ❧	Several acres
ADMISSION ❧	Fee
WHEN TO VISIT ❧	October 1 through May 31 daily, noon–4; closed
	Thanksgiving, Christmas, and New Year's;
	reservations necessary
HIGHLIGHTS ❧	11 greenhouses display plants from around the
	world; lush grounds
FACILITIES ❧	Rest room

Duke Gardens is a wonderful place to visit when it's raining or freezing outdoors: Inside 11 elaborate greenhouses you'll find a variety of environments, from the lush foliage of a tropical jungle, to an English summer garden, to the arid beauty of an American desert. Each greenhouse has a different theme; the unbelievable array of colors and aromas will keep you warm even on the coldest day.

Tobacco magnate James Buchanan Duke purchased this land in 1893 for the then huge sum of $32,680, adding many more land parcels to his holdings over the next 20 years. Duke spent over $10 million to landscape the estate; in order to move the soil from one place to another, a narrow-gauge railroad was built on the grounds, and 32 miles of track were laid over the newly-formed hills. Water drawn from the Raritan River filled a chain of nine man-made lakes and 35 ornamental fountains. Two million shrubs and specimen trees from all over the world were planted, and Italian immigrants built stone walls to encircle the vast estate. After seven years the grounds were finally complete, and

Duke began inviting people to visit and admire his creation.

Following Duke's death in 1925, the estate ceased to be maintained in the same grand style. But several years later his only child, Doris, moved to the estate after her marriage. She added an indoor skeet shoot, a Japanese garden, a boxwood garden, and an 18-hole golf course, as well as a pair of seals in one of the lakes and strolling peacocks that roamed the lawn. During World War II the property began to deteriorate once again as most of the staff entered the army. In 1958 Doris—who by now had divorced and retained her maiden name—began restoring the gardens; in 1964 she opened them to the public.

Upon arrival, you'll be whisked uphill by bus for the start of a 1-hour, 1-mile walking tour through the interconnected greenhouses. You'll begin with the romantic Italian Garden, typical of those in vogue in Europe during the 19th century. From there, you'll view a Colonial Garden filled with dazzling camellias, azaleas, magnolias, and crepe myrtles, similar to gardens found in South Carolina; an Edwardian Garden, a replica of the English home conservatory housing rare tropical plants and orchids popular in our country in the 1890s; and a French Garden, featuring 18th-century-style latticework.

Farther along, the English Garden is divided into five sections: a topiary garden, a rock garden, herbaceous borders, an herbal knot garden, and a collection of succulents. The Desert Garden, with its huge century plant and blooming prickly pear and jade, is striking, as is the Chinese Garden, containing bold rock formations, bamboo, and golden carp that swim lazily beneath the surface of a small pond. There is also a peaceful Japanese Garden.

You'll be greeted by the rich aroma of orange blossoms in the Indo-Persian Garden, while the Tropical Garden evokes the heady atmosphere of a rain forest. The Semitropical Garden features tree ferns from the volcanic high-plateau regions of New Zealand and Hawaii, and dozens of eye-catching bird-of-paradise plants.

Ms. Duke died in 1993 at age 80. Let's hope that her 2,700-acre estate and the gardens and greenhouses she developed will remain forever for all to enjoy.

NOTES: Cameras and high-heeled shoes aren't permitted. The tour is not suitable for handicapped persons. Visitors are required to follow a tour guide and may not wander freely about the estate.

49
Frank G. Helyar Woods

LOCATION ❦ Middlesex County
Rutgers University/Cook College Campus
Ryders Lane
New Brunswick 08901
732-932-9271

GARDEN SIZE ❦ 41 acres

ADMISSION ❦ No charge

WHEN TO VISIT ❦ Dawn to dusk daily, year-round

HIGHLIGHTS ❦ Chestnut graveyard, pine tree grove, Christmas tree plantation

FACILITIES ❦ None

This beautiful mixed-hardwood forest, named in memory of Dr. Frank G. Helyar, Director of Resident Instruction at Rutgers College of Agriculture from 1927 to 1953, is used for teaching, research, and demonstration purposes. Formerly owned by the Phelps family, earlier settlers to this area, the forest has survived practically undisturbed—a miracle, since it adjoins Route 1, one of the state's most heavily traveled highways. The public is welcome to enjoy the easy, level trail that begins opposite the parking area and log cabin; it's a 1.1-mile round-trip loop. The trees are numbered, but the leaflets describing the various stops are often not available; it's best to bring along a tree identification book.

The moment you enter these cool, damp, shaded woods, you'll see a huge black oak to the left. Farther along is a chestnut graveyard; one of the largest remaining stumps in this section measures 37.5 inches in diameter. Over 45 different species of trees characteristic of both upland and bottomland sites are found here. They include the tree of heaven, princess tree, yellow birch, swamp white oak, red oak, and hickory. Ahead, to the right, are mature, 90-foot-tall black and white oaks, a remnant of the original or primeval oak forest that have reached their maximum size and density. In the wet, saucerlike low areas are wetland survivors, including swamp white oak, red maple, and black gum, and various shrubs such as greenbrier, arrowwood, wild elderberry, spicebush, and jewelweed. The cinnamon ferns and skunk cabbages also love the wet ground here.

This is a great place for bird-watching; you'll be serenaded all along the trail. After a short uphill section, you'll come upon what's referred to as the Indian Cave, actually an old exploratory copper prospecting shaft. You'll find a prime example of Brunswick shale that was deposited about 160 million years ago during the Triassic Period. Iron compounds give the shale its red color; on the downhill side of the cave there's a perfect example of erosion. Once shale is exposed to the weather, it crumbles and disintegrates quite rapidly. Many plants have colonized this barren, exposed area; the algae and lichens appeared first; then the mosses; and finally, the ferns took over.

Weston's Mill Pond, a reservoir on Lawrence Brook, can be seen from the trail. Covering 92 acres, the original dam was constructed around 1860 to furnish water power for a mill operated by Colonel Weston. Eighteen species of fish live here, including largemouth bass, pickerel, perch, and sunfish. Kingfishers, green herons, osprey, and ducks can often be spotted on the pond.

50
Gail Shollar Memorial Garden

LOCATION ❧ Middlesex County
Quibbletown Park on Academy Street
Piscataway 08854
732-562-2382

GARDEN SIZE ❧ Less than ¼ acre

ADMISSION ❧ No charge

WHEN TO VISIT ❧ Dawn to dusk daily during spring and summer.

HIGHLIGHTS ❧ Scented flowers for the blind; herbs; good bird-watching in the garden and surrounding woods

FACILITIES ❧ Benches, handicapped-accessible children's playground

The Gail Shollar Memorial Garden may be the only garden of its kind in the Garden State, for it is dedicated to a woman who was kidnapped, raped, and murdered in the fall of 1992. According to Piscataway Councilwoman Helen Merolia, township officials planned the garden not as a reminder of Ms. Shollar's suffering, but as a place where flowers, representing life, are renewed each year.

A plaque in memory of Ms. Shollar was placed in 1995 in the fragrance garden, where sight-impaired children and others have the opportunity to enjoy aromatic flowers. The memorial garden itself is located in the center of an innovative "all-children's playground," designed to be accessible to those who are disabled and use wheelchairs, walkers, or canes. Dogwoods, cherry trees, and heavily scented flowers surround the main section of the playground, where a spongy rubber base has been installed to protect children who may fall; three satellite areas are covered with wood chips.

Enjoy the garden's herbs, including lemon thyme, lamb's ear, and

Asters at the Gail Shollar Memorial Garden

chives, and the plantings of yarrow, aster, hostas, lilies, and Japanese bloodgrass. Let your children romp on the barrier-free swings, jungle gyms, mini-railroad, and carousel. Relax on a bench while taking in the soothing scene, or bird-watch in the surrounding woods beneath birch, beech, and sweetgum within sight of large stands of rhododendron and azalea. And, while you enjoy this special garden, think of how lucky we are to be alive.

51

Rudolf W. van der Goot Rose Garden

LOCATION ❧	Somerset County
	Colonial Park
	Mettler's Road
	East Millstone 08873
	908-234-2677; 732-873-2459
GARDEN SIZE ❧	1 acre
ADMISSION ❧	No charge
WHEN TO VISIT ❧	*Garden:* Spring through fall, daily 10 AM–dusk. *Colonial Park:* Dawn to dusk daily, year-round. Roses are in peak bloom during June and September.
HIGHLIGHTS ❧	Rose Garden, Fragrance and Sensory Garden; over 80 varieties of annuals, perennials, herbs, flowering shrubs and vines; plant labels printed in Braille and script in the Fragrance and Sensory Garden.
FACILITIES ❧	*Garden:* Barrier-free with a wheelchair ramp and guide rail in the sunken Fragrance and Sensory Garden; benches. *Colonial Park:* Par course fitness circuit, picnicking, children's playgrounds, ponds for fishing, open play fields, rest room, drinking water.
EVENTS ❧	Rose Day in June. Call for schedule.

The Rudolf W. van der Goot Rose Garden is one of 24 nationwide test gardens sanctioned by All-America Rose Selections, Inc. (AARS), a nonprofit organization founded in 1938 by leading rose growers. The garden, established in 1971, was designed and developed by Rudolph

W. van der Goot, an industrialist who served as the Somerset County Park Commission's first horticulturist. Since receiving accreditation by the AARS in 1973—an honor reserved for gardens whose roses have passed a two-year test for bloom, disease resistance, and adaptability—the garden is privileged to display award-winning rose varieties a year before they're available for purchase by the public.

This 1-acre enclosure, located within 467-acre Colonial Park, features over 4,000 bushes of more than 275 different species of roses, and has gained a reputation as one of the 10 top rose gardens in the nation. Represented are lush displays of hybrid teas, grandifloras, floribundas, climbers, miniatures, shrubs, Old Gardens, and botanical roses. Steeped in history, roses are frequently named to honor important individuals and events. Some of the names you'll find here include 'Mister Lincoln', 'Tiffany', 'Chrysler Imperial', 'Fragrant Cloud', 'Iceberg', 'Simplicity', 'City of New York', 'Dolly Parton', and 'Barbara Bush'.

For an overall view of the three-sectioned garden, begin at the gazebo, located just past the entrance gate. Miniature roses adorn the base of a large fountain, and hybrid tea roses fill the geometric beds surrounding it. Despite the fact that many of the hybrid perpetual and hybrid tea roses found in the garden date back to the 1820s, they're considered mere infants in the lineage, since roses have been cultivated in Greece and the Orient for at least 4,000 years. It's believed that cultivated roses originated from the dog rose, (*Rosa canina*), a theory substantiated by 35 million-year-old fossils found in Montana and other areas.

The Center Garden, lined with beds of rambling, low-growing polyantha roses, is flanked by the Millicent Fenwick Rose Walk, a brick path built to honor the late US Representative and UN Ambassador. Although not a gardener, Ms. Fenwick resided in Somerset County and was the director of the New Jersey Division of Consumer Affairs.

The compact Dutch Garden section, resembling Holland's formal rose gardens, allows close viewing of dwarf candytuft, which lines beds filled with heritage roses. Until November's first frost, a few of the 80 varieties of annuals, herbs, perennials, flowering shrubs, and vines, all chosen for their rich fragrance and texture, may still be in bloom in the Fragrance and Sensory Garden in the western portion of the Rose Garden.

NOTE: Don't leave without exploring Colonial Park. The barrier-free arboretum, a living tree museum, is a delight to explore during any season. The trees, all labeled, include dwarf conifers, lilacs, and Japanese cherries, in addition to hollies, dogwoods, and viburnums. Until frost, the unusual fruiting sweetleaf shrub sports bright sapphire-blue berries. There's also a fitness circuit and a 1.4-mile bike path, and Powder Mill Pond and Mettler's Pond are good places for bird watching. Plan on spending an entire day, but don't forget to bring a picnic lunch; restaurants are a distance away.

52
Garden for the Blind and Physically Handicapped

LOCATION ❧ Middlesex County
1081 Green Street at the Iselin Library
Iselin 08830
732-283-1200 (library)
732-634-6760 (garden club)

GARDEN SIZE ❧ Less than ¼ acre

ADMISSION ❧ No charge

WHEN TO VISIT ❧ Dawn to dusk daily, year-round

HIGHLIGHTS ❧ Barrier-free with sensory, rock, and rose gardens

FACILITIES ❧ Rest room and water only during library hours

The tiny Garden for the Blind and Physically Handicapped offers visitors of all ages and capabilities an opportunity to experience the sights, smells, sounds, and textures of a garden through all of the senses. This unique barrier-free garden, maintained by the Woodbridge Garden Club, was built by the local Lions Club in 1974.

A terraced section contains the Circle of Senses Garden. Here, huge, waist-high planters are filled with aromatic herbs such as English thyme, spearmint, oregano, and basil. The abundant annuals include impatiens, colorful ornamental Scotch kale, and lavender. Each June, when vast areas of hostas, irises, and roses spring up, there are enough blooms to brighten up the dreariest day. A striking weeping willow stands near the rock garden, and the entire area is surrounded by sweet-gum and oaks.

53
Rutgers Display Gardens

LOCATION ❧ Middlesex County
Rutgers, the State University/Cook College
Ryders Lane
New Brunswick 08901
732-932-9271

GARDEN SIZE ❧ Approximately 75 acres

ADMISSION ❧ No charge

WHEN TO VISIT ❧ Daily, 8:30 AM–dusk

HIGHLIGHTS ❧ One of the largest collections of American hollies
in the world; water conservation garden; small
tree and shade tree collections; magnificent
annual flower display

FACILITIES ❧ Some garden paths are handicapped-accessible

EVENTS ❧ Annual Open House in midsummer and autumn.
Call for schedule.

It's easy to tune out the hum of traffic along Routes 1 and 18 while
you explore this lush garden. Garden buffs and nature lovers—and those
who simply like to stroll in lovely surroundings—will enjoy the color
and serenity to be found at the Rutgers Display Gardens. Here, students
learn about applied research in plant breeding, genetics, and horticulture techniques; visitors are welcome year-round.

The garden was established in 1929 with a shrub border planted for
teaching and research purposes and public outreach; today it is supported by the Friends of Rutgers Gardens and is maintained by a dedicated group of students and volunteers. Thousands of species and
cultivars, both native and introduced, cover these 75 acres, home to one
of the largest collections of American hollies in the world. Approximately 140 varieties are growing in the American Holly Variety Trials
Section, including those first used and hybridized by Rutgers/Cook

College professor, Dr. Elwin Orton. This successful endeavor resulted in the 'Jersey Knight' and 'Jersey Princess' specimens. Dr. Orton also produced cultivars of Japanese holly in 1964, identified by its spineless leaves, which are in the Japanese Holly Variety Trials Section.

Visitors return year after year to the Donald B. Lacey Annual Display Garden, added in 1965 and open from June through October. It features a sea of colorful mixed annuals and related bedding plants, along with a fine display of All-America Rose Selections. An open house, with educational talks presented by students and professors, is held in this area during midsummer and again in the fall.

Nearby are the Ella Quimby Water Conservation Gardens, a gift to the college from Rutgers alumnus Josephine Nicholson in memory of her mother, who loved gardening. Designed and built by Cook College landscape architecture students Eric Goldstein and Lars Lilientha, it consists of a series of terraces, each featuring a different drought-tolerant plant. The terraces frame the entrance to the evergreen gardens, where pine, cedar, juniper, spruce, and fir trees were planted in 1958.

Hundreds of azaleas and rhododendrons—especially striking from late April through mid-June—spread beneath a canopy of mature oak and flowering dogwood. The numerous birch, Japanese maple, flowering cherry, small magnolia, and flowering crab apple trees are a wonderful sight in late May and June.

54
William L. Hutcheson Memorial Forest

LOCATION ❧ Somerset County
Amwell Road (Route 514)
Franklin Township 08823
732-932-3388

GARDEN SIZE ❧ 155 acres

ADMISSION ❧ No charge

WHEN TO VISIT ❧ Guided tours are held on Sunday afternoons year-round, or by appointment. Call for details.

HIGHLIGHTS ❧ Designated a National Natural Area Landmark, this is a partial virgin forest untouched for over three centuries.

FACILITIES ❧ None

EVENTS ❧ Sunday-afternoon guided hikes led by Rutgers University faculty covering topics on ecology, wildlife, plants, and ornithology. Call for a schedule.

Designated as a National Natural Area Landmark by the United States National Park Service, the William L. Hutcheson Memorial Forest, one of the oldest known natural forests in North America, has specimen trees over three centuries old, and is one of the last uncut stands of hardwood trees in the eastern United States. Hikes led by ornithologists, botanists, zoologists, and wildlife biologists on the Rutgers faculty are held throughout the year on Sunday afternoons. Don't miss the opportunity to participate in a 1–2-hour guided tour through 15 acres winding through the eastern edge of this singular forest; on the return loop, you'll see a virgin forest untouched by human hands.

The forest will remain untouched in the future, thanks to concerned citizens and the Brotherhood of Carpenters and Joiners who, in 1954, successfully stopped proposed timbering plans by raising funds to purchase the land. It was then named in honor of a former union president and deeded to Rutgers, the State University, with the stipulation that should the university intervene in the course of natural events or harm the tract, the land will be immediately transferred to The Nature Conservancy or one of the other conservation groups listed in the deed.

White, black, and red oaks dominate these woods. Many stand 80 to 100 feet high, and rings from one fallen oak indicate that it originated here in 1621! There are also American beech estimated to be about 200 years old, as well as numerous mature hickories. Below the hardwood canopy are flowering dogwood and an understory of spicebush and maple-leaf viburnum. In addition, over 500 species of plants have been recorded here, including the mayapple, an early-spring bloomer. This is also a bird paradise; over 300 species of birds have been seen here, including the great horned owl, red-bellied woodpecker, white-eyed vireo, scarlet tanager, and wood thrush. There's also a healthy population of coyotes, foxes, moles, rabbits, skunks, and woodchucks.

Over the years, many changes have occurred in this forest. In the 1950s, when the multiflora rose was planted as a median buffer on highways, it attracted mockingbirds, which began wintering here. In 1955, a strong hurricane hit, toppling several trees and introducing new species like the ailanthus. Gypsy moths defoliated the forest in the late 1980s, which let in more sunlight to the understory and allowed non-native species like Japanese honeysuckle to gain a foothold.

According to Dr. Edmund Stiles, a professor in the Department of Ecology, Evolution, and Natural Resources at Rutgers, "This tract is better studied than perhaps any other plot in the world. It is actually a climax forest, meaning that the trees have reached the oldest age they can reach and are now replacing themselves naturally." This is an ideal place to witness forest succession first-hand; here, when older trees die, they're left to decay as part of the natural cycle. Professors and students at Rutgers are also engaged in continuous research projects in the forest focusing on plant growth, food preferences of the native wildlife and birds, and annual migration habits.

55
Buccleuch Mansion Gardens

LOCATION ❧	Middlesex County
	Buccleuch Park
	Easton Avenue opposite St. Peter's Hospital
	New Brunswick 08901
	732-745-5094
GARDEN SIZE ❧	Less than 2 acres
ADMISSION ❧	No charge
WHEN TO VISIT ❧	*Garden:* Dawn to dusk, daily. Peak bloom for peonies and cherry trees is late May.
	House: Open from 2–4 on Sundays, June through October; private tours available at other times by reservation.
HIGHLIGHTS ❧	Old boxwoods, roses, lilacs, and geometric flower beds planted with over 6,000 annuals; historic manor house
FACILITIES ❧	Rest room, benches

Ancient boxwood and lilac shrubs over 200 years old surround this unique garden, which is divided into geometric flower beds that are filled each summer with thousands of annuals. One of the garden's most unusual features are the Elizabethan viewing mounds, created by heaping soil into small hills. A common feature on estates like this in the 1700s, according to curator Sue Cannon, they were constructed to allow a better view of the plantings. One mound is situated by the sundial in the middle of the garden, while the other two can be found by the weeping cherry trees on either side of the garden.

But it's also possible to appreciate this garden at ground level via the wide, winding paths that allow passage through most areas. The garden was originally designed by Colonel John Scott in the early 1800s; his lilacs and part of his original sundial remain. The garden eventually fell into ruin, and was restored in the 1970s by the Daughters of the American Revolution. In addition to the attractive weeping cherry trees, plantings include fragrant roses in the old-fashioned-rose section, a modern rose bed, climbing roses, a rustic arbor adorned with wisteria, a living wall of forsythia and shrubs, a tall border of perennial flowers, a medium border with ancient peonies, and a low border featuring chrysanthemums in the fall.

Plan on visiting when the house is open for tours, since the entire property—now part of Buccleuch Park—is steeped in history. Originally known as White House Farm, its first owners—Anthony Walton White and his wife, the daughter of Governor Lewis Morris—held a high social position and frequently entertained guests, such as George Washington and Alexander Hamilton, inside their stately 1739 mansion as well as outside on the vast lawn area that extended to the river's edge. When Colonel Joseph Warren Scott, a New Jersey attorney, purchased the property in 1821, he changed the name of the estate to Buccleuch in honor of his ancestor, the duke of Buccleuch in Scotland.

In 1911, his heirs gave the mansion and surrounding acres to the City of New Brunswick for use as a public park. The house, also refurbished by the Daughters of the American Revolution, provides an excellent peek at the past and a look at a vast array of period furniture and rare woods.

NOTE: Feel free to bring a picnic lunch to enjoy in the park, where the lawn area is also perfect for tossing a Frisbee or playing catch.

56
Rockingham Herb Garden

LOCATION ❧ Somerset County
Route 518, east of Rocky Hill
Princeton 08540
609-921-8835

GARDEN SIZE ❧ Less than ¼ acre

ADMISSION ❧ *Gardens:* No charge. *House:* Fee.

WHEN TO VISIT ❧ *Garden:* Dawn to dusk daily, spring through fall.
House: Wednesday through Saturday, 10–noon
and 1–4; Sunday, 1–4, August through
November. Closed major holidays.

HIGHLIGHTS ❧ 18th-century herb garden adjoining a house used
by General George Washington

FACILITIES ❧ Rest room and water when the building is open.

Plan to visit this charming herb garden in combination with a visit to Rockingham, a 20-room farmhouse built in the 1730s. The small herb garden at the rear of the house contains many of the herbs used during Colonial times for flavoring vegetables and meat, dyeing clothing, repelling insects, or for perfume. The gardens at the side of the house also contain many flowers that would have been there in the 1730s, including the Madonna lily, cornflower, candytuft, and peony.

Walk along the brick path leading through the herb garden, and check out the vegetables planted in back of the house near the herbs. You'll find cabbage, sugar snap peas, eggplant, and lima beans here, as well as hens-and-chicks, a succulent ground cover now taking over the nooks in the rocks.

The original house, constructed in 1710 in the New England Colonial style, had a dining room and upstairs study, but when John Berrien purchased it in the 1730s, he named the house Rockingham and enlarged it to 20 rooms. He sold the house in 1783, along with

The Rockingham Herb Garden adjoins a house used by General George Washington.

360 acres consisting of orchards, farmland, and woodland, complete with a barn, stables, coach house, granary, fowl house, kitchen building, smokehouse, and a three-room tenement house.

Shortly thereafter, General George Washington arrived with his wife, Martha, and a few troops; he delivered his farewell address to the troops here on November 7, 1783. They used the large Blue Room on the second floor as a study, and the two small adjoining rooms for a bedroom and dressing room. During their stay Washington and Martha entertained many prominent guests on the grounds, including Alexander Hamilton, Thomas Jefferson, James Madison, and Richard Stockton. Often, when too many guests were invited, they dined beneath a marquee erected on the spacious lawn.

The property changed hands many times through the years, and when it was threatened with destruction in the late 1800s, concerned citizens formed the Washington Headquarters Association, collected the necessary funds to buy it, and proceeded to move the house a short distance. After restoring the house, the group opened it to visitors in 1897. The state received the house as a gift from the association in 1935, but it had to be moved a short distance once again in 1957 to protect it from nearby quarry blasting. The present gardens were planted in the 1960s by the Stoney Brook Garden Club of Princeton and are maintained today by the same group.

57
Prallsville Industrial Herb Garden

LOCATION ❧ Hunterdon County
Route 29
Stockton 08559
609-397-3223; 609-258-3455

GARDEN SIZE ❧ Less than ½ acre

ADMISSION ❧ No charge

WHEN TO VISIT ❧ *Garden:* Dawn to dusk daily. *Buildings:* Open only when an event is scheduled.

HIGHLIGHTS ❧ Herb garden containing plants that had industrial uses from early times to the present. Part of the Delaware and Raritan Canal State Park, the complex is listed on the National Register of Historic Places.

FACILITIES ❧ Rest room when buildings are open; picnic table along the canal

EVENTS ❧ Herb sale; horticultural meetings; lectures, concerts, regional festivals.

The Prallsville Mills Industrial Herb Garden, situated next to the Delaware and Raritan Canal, is one of only three such gardens in the country (the others are located at the National Arboretum in Washington, D.C., and the Brooklyn Botanic Garden in New York). Established in 1986 by the Delaware Valley Herb Unit of the Herb Society of America, this small, lovely garden contains only those plants that had industrial uses from Colonial times to the present. The demonstration plantings contain plants that were used by housewives making their own clothing, medicines, and fragrances before the advent of factories. Adjacent to the garden are a gristmill, a stone linseed-oil mill, a sawmill, a stable, and a granary; the towpath along the canal is perfect for a stroll. The garden, shaded by an overhead sweetgum canopy, is arranged in sections according to use: Medicinal, Fragrance, Flax, Field Crops, Dye Pit, and Household. Many of the plants here—such as rice, hops, bedstraw, and alfalfa—are not found at other historic sites.

Useful plants in the Medicinal Section include borage, used for fever, to strengthen the eyes and to increase milk production; butterfly weed, a Native American medicine; autumn crocus, a source of colchicine, a powerful drug used to treat gout; coneflower, used to enhance healing and immunity to infection; foxglove, a source of the heart medication digitalis; Lady's mantle, a veterinary medicine for diarrhea; evening primrose, used to increase immunity; the apothecary rose, for colds, headaches, and palpitations; American senna, a purgative; thyme, used in worm medication; and witch hazel, distilled for use in astringent preparations, salves, and lotions.

The Fragrance plantings are used in potpourri, soap, powders, and perfume. They include scented geraniums, wild ginger, hyssop, lavender, lemon verbena, gray santolina, sweet flag, rosemary, and orris root, among others. The Household area contains a huge variety of useful plants; bayberry leaves were used to make candles and to freshen linens; chicory was used as a coffee substitute; and horehound flavored candy and cough syrups.

The Field Crops section includes food crops such as anise, blue corn, and buckwheat. Sesame oil is used for both culinary and industrial purposes, and the seed heads of broom corn were used to make brooms and whisk brooms. The Fibers section contains flax, which was used for fabric, rope, and thread; the oil from its seeds is used in paint and soap, and as a laxative in veterinary medicine. Papyrus is also used for paper and rope. In addition to being raised for its fibers, the oil from cotton seeds is used in food and soap manufacturing.

Prallsville is steeped in history, for Daniel Howell built a gristmill here between the Wichecheoke Creek and the Delaware River long before the American Colonies declared themselves a free nation. The mill prospered through the 18th century under a series of owners. After John Prall Jr. purchased the property in 1794, he built a new stone gristmill to replace the wooden one built by Howell, added a sawmill, several stone houses, a stone linseed oil mill, a plaster mill, a chapel, a post office, and a store, in addition to operating a stone quarry and two fisheries in the Delaware River.

When operations ceased here in the 1950s, the property quickly deteriorated. When it was in danger of being demolished to make way for townhouses, local resident Donald B. Jones saved it by purchasing

Prallsville Industrial Herb Garden

the property and selling it to the state in 1973. It was placed on the National Register of Historic Places that same year and, in 1974, became part of the Delaware and Raritan Canal State Park. Today, the Delaware River Mill Society has the responsibility of restoring, preserving, operating, maintaining, and interpreting the state-owned Prallsville Mills, the only surviving 19th-century village industrial complex on the Delaware and Raritan Canal.

NOTE: Bring a picnic lunch to enjoy along the canal; take a short or long stroll along this lovely waterway; or hike the 15 miles of abandoned railroad line that runs from Lambertville to Frenchtown and passes through the mill site.

58
Johnson Ferry House Kitchen Garden

LOCATION ❧ Mercer County
Washington Crossing State Park
355 Washington Crossing and Pennington Road
Titusville 08560
609-737-2515 (garden)
609-737-9304 (visitors center)

GARDEN SIZE ❧ Pocket-sized

ADMISSION ❧ No charge

WHEN TO VISIT ❧ Wednesday through Saturday 10–4:30; 1–4:30 Sunday. Closed Mondays, Tuesdays and holidays.

HIGHLIGHTS ❧ 18th-century kitchen garden with vast array of herbs and old-fashioned roses; circa-1740 ferry house on a historic site

FACILITIES ❧ Rest room and water in park; the garden and the first floor of the house are partially handicapped-accessible.

EVENTS ❧ Concerts in the garden; living history demonstrations; Flax Day; Harvest Feast. Call for a schedule.

Today the Johnson Ferry House kitchen garden is much smaller than when Rutger Jansen and his family lived here in the 1740s, but it's a good example of a typical kitchen garden of that era. Located outside the front door, kitchen gardens provided plants used for food, clothing, medicine, dyes, and perfumes. Most likely it wasn't as pretty at that time as it is today, either, for kitchen gardens were not ornamental but were planted for purely practical purposes.

In recent years, park personnel and volunteers have gradually changed the Colonial garden created here in 1926 by the Daughters of the American Revolution to a design similar to the gardens established by immigrants from the Netherlands during the 18th century. Attractive brick walkways lend a feeling of warmth and lead to numerous planting areas and a sundial installed by the DAR. Often a basket of squash or fresh-picked vegetables can be found at its base.

According to caretaker Nancy Carter, since kitchen gardens in the 1740s were often invaded by animals, they were usually surrounded by fencing: "Raised beds within these gardens would be filled with edible plants, such as salad greens, radishes, turnips, carrots, cabbages, watermelons, and broccoli. However, members of the nightshade family—tomatoes, eggplants, green peppers, and even potatoes—wouldn't be found in gardens of that era because they were thought to be sinful. Potatoes were eaten by poor families in Europe long before they were accepted in the family garden here."

Perennial plants ring the perimeter of the garden. In addition to herbs, you'll find the same flowers that the lady of the house would have chosen, such as hollyhocks, the 1880 Damask rose of Castile, the apothecary rose, and a number of other rose varieties dating from 1750 or before. Roses during that period tended to be smaller and had a sweeter fragrance than do the hybrid roses of today.

Although a demonstration bed of flax is now located in one corner of the garden, it was normally planted outside the kitchen garden by the acre to yield thread for linen and rug batting. A Native American patch planted with corn, pumpkins, and gourds is in another part of the kitchen garden, but this, too, would have been planted outside the garden walks. A skep, used to attract bees, is near a shade arbor adorned with wisteria.

Take time for the interesting scheduled tour of the Ferry House. It's believed that the Continental Army landed here under General George Washington's command after their historic crossing of the Delaware River in 1776, and that Washington spent some time inside the house. Today, it's furnished with Colonial pieces appropriate to the time when it was the ferry keeper's residence.

NOTE: Take along a picnic lunch to enjoy in the park; there are numerous picnic tables, grills, and stone fireplaces. The visitors center has an exhibit of over 900 artifacts from the Revolutionary War era. Within the park there's a mountain bike trail, 13 miles of hiking trails, and a nature center.

59
Herrontown Woods Arboretum

LOCATION ❀ Mercer County
Snowden Lane near Herrontown Road junction
Princeton 08540
609-989-6530

GARDEN SIZE ❀ Several acres

ADMISSION ❀ No charge

WHEN TO VISIT ❀ Dawn to dusk daily, year-round

HIGHLIGHTS ❀ A pine forest; more than 30 species of trees;
outstanding wildflowers during spring; great bird-watching

FACILITIES ❀ Marked trails

Herrontown Woods Arboretum is a place to wander slowly. Search for wildflowers, make rubbings of the tree bark, listen to the birds, or simply enjoy the solitude, only minutes from the Princeton University campus.

The late Professor Oswald Veblen found his 142-acre estate such a source of enjoyment and relaxation that he donated it to the Mercer County Park Commission in 1957 so that others could also be enriched by its peaceful surroundings. The grounds include a pine forest, over 30 species of trees, a variety of shrubs, and dozens of wildflowers, including jack-in-the-pulpits, violets, and marsh buttercups.

Marked trails start at the parking lot where a trail map is posted. Don't get discouraged when you pass an ugly steel fence on your right just after starting out; it disappears in a few minutes as you soon enter an area with an old barn and farmhouse. A bronze plaque set onto a rock thanks the professor and his wife for their generous gift of land.

During winter months, the maple's red branches stand out, while the beech supports dried golden leaves that cling tightly as though afraid to fall. Oaks decorate the top of the ridge. Nearby is the sweet gum—named for a sticky substance that oozes from cuts made in the branches or trunk—but you won't have to look up to see it; you'll be stepping on the one-inch round seed clusters it drops in autumn when its star-shaped leaves turn bright crimson and orange. Tulip trees tower majestically overhead; if you have a magnifying glass, you can examine the beautiful green and gray lichens adorning the huge boulders.

A small stream along the yellow-blazed trail is a nice spot to relax and reflect upon nature. You might want to bring a butterfly identification book along; they seem to love these woods. Walk softly on the way back to your car; you might spot a few of the white-tailed deer that have made the arboretum their home.

60
Marquand Park

LOCATION ❧ Mercer County
Lovers Lane
Princeton 08540
609-921-9480

GARDEN SIZE ❧ 17 acres

ADMISSION ❧ No charge

WHEN TO VISIT ❧ Dawn to dusk daily, year-round.

HIGHLIGHTS ❧ 200 species of domestic and foreign trees; 11 trees are the largest of their kind in the state.

FACILITIES ❧ Handicapped-accessible; paved walks, playground, picnic area, ball field

Accessible in Princeton from footpaths off Stockton Street, Mercer Street, and from a parking lot on Lovers Lane, lies Marquand Park, a beautiful 17-acre tract consisting of woodlands, forest glades, and open parkland. Visitors to this horticultural gem will find wide expanses of lawn and a variety of specimen trees and shrubs that date to the 19th century, a time when explorers traveled the world seeking unusual plantings to adorn the estates of the wealthy.

Judge Richard Field, a professor of jurisprudence at Princeton University, was largely responsible for the creation of this outstanding arboretum, a living museum of shrubs and trees from around the world. After purchasing 30 acres of farmland in 1842, including the present land the park occupies, he built his residence, Guernsey Hall, but first, he spent 10 years designing the grounds. With the help of William Petrey, an English gardener, Field transplanted local trees and rare species obtained in the United States and abroad, among them incense cedars from the Sierra Nevadas, Norway spruces, cedars imported from Lebanon, and European larches.

In 1871, the property was sold to Susan Brown. In a very short time,

Marquand Park, featuring 200 species of domestic and foreign trees, is the perfect place to listen to the birds.

her son developed a well-deserved reputation for eccentricity among Princeton University students: In order to protect his mother's roses from trespassers, he built a high wooden fence and patrolled the property with a shotgun. He also contributed greatly to the estate's collection by planting many Japanese maples and a massive Amur cork tree.

When Princeton professor Allan Marquand acquired the property in 1885, he and his wife continued adding to the collection. Mrs. Marquand lived here until her death in 1950; thanks to the generosity of the Marquand heirs, 17 acres were donated to the borough in 1953 to be used as a public park, playground, and recreational area. A nonprofit foundation was organized to provide for the property, and since that time more than 100 species have been added.

As you enter the park you see an outstanding empress tree, the largest of its species in New Jersey; during early spring, it's covered with pale-violet blossoms. Along the footpath you'll find a small kobus magnolia, and firs from Syria and Greece. At the junction where the path branches, look for a threadleaf Japanese maple, with its amazingly contorted form. During fall, its fernlike leaves turn a bright bronze. East of this tree sits a huge white oak with wide spreading branches and, to the south, near the boundary of the park where the privately owned Guernsey Hall residence stands, is the striking cedar of Lebanon that

Field planted in 1842 when the tree was 10 feet high and 7 years old.

In the northern corner of the park you'll find the dawn redwood, a deciduous conifer with bright-green to bluish-green leaves, that was thought to be extinct until a living tree was discovered in China in 1945. Its seeds were distributed worldwide, and a Princeton University horticulturist planted one here in 1955.

You'll find an Oriental spruce on the northwest park boundary, another of the largest of its species in New Jersey. Nearby is a blue Atlas cedar, identified by distinctive blue-green needles growing in clusters of 7–10 on short spurs. Explore the eastern section of the park along Mercer Street; it supports natural woodlands where the oldest trees can be found, including tulip, beech, hickory, oak, and maple.

NOTE: Bring binoculars. Woodpeckers, chickadees, titmice, cardinals, bluejays, and juncos frequent the park year-round. Princeton University is only a few minutes away; the campus, dotted with a variety of trees and sculpture, is wonderful to stroll around.

61

Prospect Gardens

LOCATION ❧	Mercer County
	Princeton University Campus
	Off Washington Road
	Princeton 08540
	609-258-3000
GARDEN SIZE ❧	Approximately 2 acres
ADMISSION ❧	No charge
WHEN TO VISIT ❧	Dawn to dusk daily, year-round
HIGHLIGHTS ❧	Extensive seasonal plants; exotic and native trees
FACILITIES ❧	Rest room; benches
EVENTS ❧	Weddings and Princeton-sponsored events. Call for schedule.

Prospect Garden has often been accurately described as a stroller's garden. Here, tucked away on Princeton University's campus, nature lovers delight in exploring this serene garden year-round.

Laid out in 1843 by an English gardener named William Petrey from plans drawn by a Canadian architect, the garden—maintained by the university's Grounds and Greenhouse foremen—appears practically the same as it did in the 18th century, when successive presidents of the university occupied the mansion overlooking these grounds. About the only changes made were by Ellen Wilson in 1879. At that time, she added a central pool, expanded the rose gardens, and had her husband—university president Woodrow Wilson—enclose the flower garden with an iron fence to protect it from students walking to classes. According to some tour guides, she also had the layout changed to resemble the Princeton seal.

Even before the first president of the university resided here—on land that was donated to Princeton in 1878 by Robert L. and Alexander Stuart—the trees, including tulip and American beech, were impressive.

Prospect Gardens, on the Princeton campus, appears much as it did during the 18th century.

Today, the tulips stand over 100 feet tall, and the 70-foot beech near the garden's entrance is truly magnificent, especially in the fall when its leaves turn deep bronze.

Additional plants, starting with the cedar of Lebanon, hawthorn, and a yew that Petrey brought in, were introduced soon after the Florentine-style mansion was completed in 1849. The impressive dawn redwood and ginkgo have been here almost as long. Other trees surrounding the garden include 19 that are native to the eastern United States, 4 to the Pacific Northwest, 2 to the Rockies, and 1 to California. The imported trees are from China, India, and Spain, and include a Japanese dogwood, Himalayan pine, and European beech.

Although the trees are magnificent, it is the flower garden that Ellen Wilson established in 1904 at the rear of Prospect Garden that draws visitors to this lovely area. Within the living fence of Canada hemlock at the perimeter of this semicircular two-level garden—which consists of central gardens, the rose gardens at the top landing, and surrounding areas of shrubs and trees—are annuals and perennial plantings in every conceivable color, laid out in geometric beds surrounding a central fountain.

Early spring brings a showing of over 3,000 daffodils, 6,000 tulips, and countless hyacinths, followed by a tremendous display of irises and peonies. During midsummer, when the annuals are set out, daylilies and mixed perennials make a spectacular appearance, and throughout the summer, lavender, iberis, hosta, and dead nettle add color and interest to the landscape. Birds, hummingbirds, and insects are drawn to the bright-red salvia, as well as to the begonias, geraniums, hostas, dusty millers, columbines, and marigolds. By autumn, chrysanthemums are added to the beautiful array. Around the formal plantings, carefully tended lawns and evergreens create the perfect backdrop.

University gardeners turn over the central gardens three times annually to remove out-of-season flowers and replace them with the upcoming season's favorites. Most of the spring annuals are raised from seed in the greenhouses, and after the fall bulbs are removed from the beds, they're replaced by elegant summer flora including impatiens, pinks, dusty millers, and coleus.

The mansion, formerly home to university presidents, is now used as a social center for faculty and staff, but you don't have to go up to the terrace to view the flowering dogwoods, azaleas, and rhododendrons. Everything is within touching distance in this special garden, where there's always something in bloom.

62
Drumthwacket Gardens

LOCATION ❧ Mercer County
354 Stockton Street (Route 206)
Princeton 08540
609-683-0057
GARDEN SIZE ❧ Approximately 12 acres
ADMISSION ❧ No charge
WHEN TO VISIT ❧ Wednesdays noon–2
HIGHLIGHTS ❧ Multi-level terrace garden; mansion
FACILITIES ❧ Rest room, water, benches

Drumthwacket's gardens are a must-see, as is touring the mansion, designated New Jersey's official gubernatorial residence in the early 1980s. Governor James Florio was one of its first residents; his wife, Lucinda, is credited with facilitating the rehabilitation of the gardens and adding a contemporary look that blends in beautifully with the original classic style. Maintained by the New Jersey Division of Parks and Forestry, the gardens are especially spectacular during spring, when the azalea, rhododendron, and magnolia burst into bloom along with hundreds of tulips and daffodils.

Before you're admitted to the garden, you'll be invited to tour the inside of the mansion. The property was originally purchased in 1696 by William Olden. His grandson, Thomas, built the small house still standing near the street, and that's where Charles Olden was born in 1799. Charles was responsible for building the Greek Revival–style main section of the mansion in the early 1830s, with its six-columned portico and Ionic columns. Olden served as a state Senator, judge, and treasurer of the College of New Jersey, now known as Princeton University; he was also New Jersey's 28th governor, during the early part of the Civil War.

Olden lived here until his death at the age of 77 in 1893; when his wife died 17 years later, the land and house were purchased by Moses

Sundial at Drumthwacket Gardens

Taylor Pyne, an alumnus and trustee of the university. Pyne added two wings to the mansion, built the exquisite wood-paneled library, and began building the lovely network of terraces and gardens in the rear. He employed 30 full-time gardeners, and constructed the three ponds filled with magnificent lotus flowers that were described by Mrs. Woodrow Wilson as "the most beautiful hues of the deepest pink to white with leaves like cradles." Pyne was responsible for naming the property Drumthwacket, which is believed to come from the Gaelic: *drum* means a hill, and *thwacket* means a thicket or wooded area. In 1966 Abram Spranel, the last owner, sold the property to the state. However, since it was used only part of each year, it fell into disrepair until its official designation as the governor's residence.

Since the plantings aren't tagged, it helps to bring along tree and flower identification guides. Near the porch you'll see stately sycamores and a privet; magnolias and birches are everywhere; and peonies can be found at the foot of the birches, along with blue salvia and impatiens throughout the property. Feel free to stroll in any direction from the lovely flagstone terrace. In June and September, the two semicircular rose beds at either end of the garden are bursting with beauties from the David Austin collection; huge buddleias attract dozens of colorful butterflies; there's a pretty sundial on the middle terrace; and don't miss the frog pond in a wooded area on the bottom terrace. The grounds also feature drystone retaining walls and benches marked with memorial plaques.

63
Quietude Garden

LOCATION ❦ Middlesex County
24 Fern Road
East Brunswick 08816
732-257-4340
E-mail: quietude24@aol.com

GARDEN SIZE ❦ 4 acres

ADMISSION ❦ No charge

WHEN TO VISIT ❦ Friday, Saturday, and Sunday noon–5, and by appointment

HIGHLIGHTS ❦ Large outdoor display garden featuring more than 150 sculptures; Japanese garden; and indoor designers' showcase

FACILITIES ❦ Rest room

EVENTS ❦ Regularly scheduled appearances by new sculptors in the garden. Call or write for a schedule.

At Quietude Garden, Edward Thau has introduced hundreds of varieties of flowers, rare plants, and many species of trees into what was originally a forest of red and white oaks, maples, and evergreens. In addition, he has turned the property into a unique park and sculpture garden. Here you'll find works in bronze, stone, marble, steel, wood, concrete, clay, and fiberglass. Ranging from traditional to abstract, the pieces are placed throughout the grounds and situated beneath trees and along the pleasant self-guiding trail.

Thau came up with his idea after a trip to England, where he and his wife enjoyed visiting a sculpture garden. After returning to New Jersey, they bought four acres of land and decided to create a sculpture garden of their own and to invite the public to browse on landscaped grounds that would also be a unique gallery of plants and sculpture.

When you visit Quietude, first stop in at the office next to the parking area. Sheila Thau is usually available to answer questions and will lend you a numbered guide to the outdoor sculpture. The trail begins near the visitor parking at the flower garden, where many of the bulbs begin blooming before the snow melts, such as the snowdrop, and the crocus. The Lenten rose, with pink and purple flowers, is also an early bloomer. In March and April, grape hyacinths and daffodils make an appearance, followed by tulips and canna lilies.

Each year, Thau plants more than 10,000 Holland bulbs throughout the grounds. The silver-queen hydrangeas remain attractive year round; their foliage turns from purple to bronze, and the summer-blooming white flowers dry and cling to the bush until they're cut in the spring. Near the house you'll find the extraordinary bonsai Thau grows, and a pair of strikingly beautiful spring-blooming dogwoods. There are also over 30 varieties of rhododendron and azalea; ten varieties of specimen hosta; five varieties of primrose; and gigantic Drumstick and New Guinea impatiens.

You'll eventually reach an attractive gazebo where people often sit and meditate or listen to the birds while admiring the annuals, perennials, and roses that bloom in this area from June through September. Further along, after crossing a pretty wooden bridge, you'll find a secluded spot with a small pond filled with ornamental koi.

During April, the Solomon's seal emerges, displaying showy, waxy-white, green-tipped bells, while the hyacinths, also early-spring arrivals, produce brilliant spikes of round purple blossoms. In the summer months, bugbane, a tall perennial that pushes its spirelike stems toward the sky, bursts open with hundreds of tiny white flowers resembling bottle brushes. The arching branches of weigela are in their glory with flowers like the foxglove's; the vivid golds of the coreopsis are everywhere; caladiums in pink, red, white, and green can be admired beneath the trees; and variegated hostas light up the forest floor.

Visit again in autumn, when the euonymus turns an extraordinary shade of pink and later crimson, rodgersia brightens up the dark woods with its bronze leaves that slowly change to copper, and the chrysanthemums are dazzling.

64
Kuser Farm Park Gardens

LOCATION ❦ Mercer County
Entrances at 390 Newkirk Avenue and
at Kuser Road
Hamilton 08650
609-890-3630

GARDEN SIZE ❦ *Mansion Formal Garden:* Less than ½ acre.
Kuser Farm Park: 28 acres.

ADMISSION ❦ No charge

WHEN TO VISIT ❦ *Garden:* Dawn to dusk daily, year-round. *Mansion:*
February through April, Saturday and Sunday
11–3; May through November, Thursday through
Sunday 11–3.

HIGHLIGHTS ❦ Kentucky coffee tree, remnants of grape vines
dating from 1892; shaded grounds; historic
mansion

FACILITIES ❦ Rest room; benches, two picnic areas, bandstand-
sized gazebo, playground

EVENTS ❦ Walking tours of the grounds; summer concerts;
outdoor Christmas holiday celebration. Call for
schedule.

Fred Kuser loved trees so much that when he purchased the original 70 acres of land on which he built this summer residence in 1892, he situated the house to avoid chopping down an ancient Kentucky coffee tree. The massive tree still stands, although in 1950 a hurricane sheared off much of its side limbs. At that time, 284 rings were counted on the downed wood of this lovely specimen, which bears fragrant, whitish flowers in late spring.

There are also numerous oaks, maples, dogwoods, and sourwoods on the grounds, plus remnants of Kuser's grape vines. The Victorian-

Kuser Farm Park Gardens include numerous oaks, maples, dogwoods, and remnants of ancient grapevines.

style formal garden in front of the mansion is filled with begonias, caladium, petunias, and ageratum. The formal garden also features roses, wisteria, fancy rhododendrons, and azaleas, plus a stone bench facing the plantings and a vast lawn where peacocks once roamed freely.

Nearby is an attractive gazebo that was designed by John Cordis of the Division of Planning and erected by the Township of Hamilton Building and Grounds crew in 1977 for the park's dedication. Used for weddings and free concerts that are open to the public throughout the summer, the gazebo is similar to one that was originally located on the large lawn to the right of the open porch of the mansion and near the driveway that circles down to the coach house. From the gazebo, surrounded by plantings of annuals, dwarf Alberta spruce, and hanging baskets filled with petunias, impatiens, and periwinkle, you'll see numerous white wooden posts. These were once part of a fence that continued down the entrance lane, which was lined with a row of stately Norway maples that separated two large vegetable fields. The trees were taken down when Kuser's son, Raymond, started using the 25-acre field as a runway for his Waco biplane.

With a brochure and map of the grounds (obtainable inside the house), you can locate the structures Kuser built after purchasing the original 70 acres for $7,000. They include chicken houses, stables, a corn crib, a barn, windmills, the coachman's house, a laundry house, a shower house, and one of the finest clay tennis courts in the state. The mansion was built by carpenters who worked at Kuser's father-in-law's New York brewery, where Kuser served as brewmaster. The carpenters' skill is evident throughout the mansion, in the matched grain, quartered oak paneling, and ornately carved fireplaces. In 1892, the Kusers had their first meal in their "county place," where they continued to return each summer. When his wife died in 1926, Kuser closed his New York house and moved here permanently. In 1931, he married Edna Howe, the daughter of a prominent nurseryman.

Kuser died in 1937 and left the farm to his four sons. His wife continued to live here until 1976, when Hamilton Township purchased the farm with the assistance of New Jersey Green Acres Funds. Today, Denise Zemlansky, supervisor of the historic site, encourages visitors to tour the inside of this fascinating mansion, where 17 of the 22 rooms on two of the three floors are authentically decorated as they were when the Kusers lived here.

65

Bristol-Myers Squibb Friendship Garden

LOCATION ❧ Middlesex County
Delaware-Raritan Girl Scout Council
108 Church Lane
East Brunswick 08816
732-821-9090
GARDEN SIZE ❧ Pocket-sized
ADMISSION ❧ No charge
WHEN TO VISIT ❧ Dawn to dusk daily, year-round
HIGHLIGHTS ❧ Charming gardens designed, planted, and
maintained by Girl Scouts
FACILITIES ❧ Rest room and water when the building is open

In the garden with all the sand,
Stands some flowers on the land.
Children come from far and wide,
To see the flowers with their pride.
Without the children's love and care,
The Friendship Garden would not be here.

—DENISE MCGLOAN

The Friendship Garden, developed with funds from the Bristol-Myers Squibb Corporation, was originally created to teach Girl Scouts of the Delaware-Raritan Girl Scout Council about flowers, trees, and shrubs and the vital role trees play in our lives. Girl Scouts can earn a New Leaf achievement patch for successfully completing the Friendship Garden patch program.

Scouts worked closely with Niki Graf, the supervisor of horticulture and greenhouses at Cook College; together they designed the iden-

Black-eyed Susan blooms in the Hot Spot Garden.

tification plaques and wrote a garden nature guide. In the spring of 1995, after Greg Hurley of the East Brunswick Parks Department prepared the ground and dug the holes for the large trees, Girl Scouts from the Spotswood Service Unit joined with volunteers, mentors, and professionals, to plant the garden. Officially dedicated in May 1996, the Bristol-Myers Squibb Friendship Garden is now maintained by cadet scouts in grades 7 through 9. The garden is neatly divided into several sections with a circular area in the middle; plants are grouped in each section according to their growing requirements.

The Front Garden, containing plants that require full sun, includes spirea, a deciduous shrub with a low, rounded form; cushion mum, a low, spreading, fall-blooming perennial; azalea; and tiger lilies. The Circle Garden glows throughout the summer with cheerful white and yellow Shasta daisies and purple coneflowers.

The Hot Spot Garden is loaded with plants that love the warmth of summer: they include black-eyed Susan, which bears orange or white daisylike blooms; coralbells, a tall spiked coral or pink bell-shaped flower that often reaches a height of 18 inches from June to September; bee balm, attractive to bees and hummingbirds when its red tubular flowers reach their peak from July to August; lupines with brick-red spikes; the graceful aromatic Russian sage with silvery gray hairs and small, whorled lavender-blue flowers; and a display of hibiscus and mixed daylilies.

In the Butterfly Garden you'll find delphiniums in blue, lavender, purple, and white growing next to painted daisies, and hybrid phlox that ranges from 6 inches to 4 feet. A field guide to butterflies will help you identify the black swallowtail, with black wings and yellow markings; the checkered skipper, dark brown with alternating white markings; and the orange and black monarch. In August, the ruby-throated hummingbird— the only hummingbird found in New Jersey—can also be seen here.

In the Endless Bloom Perennial Garden, hardy primroses bloom in pink, red, yellow, scarlet, purple, and white in early spring. Gaillardia's gold, red, and brown flowers bloom from early summer to frost. Here, too, is the long-lasting Siberian iris; red, pink, yellow, and maroon hollyhocks; luminous pink peonies; and an assortment of woolly speedwells, black-eyed Susans, daisies, and begonias.

In the Rear Garden a 'Hetzii' juniper displays blue foliage year-round; coreopsis, also referred to as tickseed, features long-flowering daisylike heads that bloom from June to the first frost. Santolina, a fragrant perennial, blooms in June and July with small spikes of yellow flowers; mixed daylilies bloom in summer, and a pretty linden tree bears tiny white and yellow flowers during summer and blue berries in late summer and fall. During spring the flowering dogwood, wildflowers, and viburnum are magnificent in this area.

66
Deep Cut Gardens

LOCATION ❧ Monmouth County
352 Red Hill Road
(east of the Garden State Parkway exit 114)
Middletown Township 07748
732-671-6050

GARDEN SIZE ❧ 52 acres

ADMISSION ❧ No charge

WHEN TO VISIT ❧ *Garden:* Daily, 8 AM–dusk, year-round. *Main building:* 8–4.

HIGHLIGHTS ❧ Rockery, perennial gardens, greenhouses filled with spectacular orchids, orchard, walking paths, aquatic garden

FACILITIES ❧ Rest room, classrooms, horticultural reference library, gift shop. Horticultural Hot Line (732-671-6906) staffed by trained horticulturists.

EVENTS ❧ Seasonal plant sales; garden-related seminars; monthly bus trips to outstanding gardens

At Deep Cut Gardens Horticultural Center, you can enjoy a casual stroll through a meadow of wildflowers, watch hummingbirds hover over colorful, nectar-bearing annuals and perennials, and admire water lilies and bog plants in a lily pond that's home to koi.

Over 100 acres were originally owned by the Taylor and Osborn families until 1907. In 1935 the property was deeded to the crime boss Vito Genovese, who renovated the old farmhouse, built extensive stone walls, and hired Italian workers to build hillside gardens, including an Italian-style rock garden on the steep slope below the house, an English boxwood garden planted with roses and annuals, and a series of ornamental pools with water supplied by a deep well. At the bottom of the garden, in addition to building a huge swimming pool, he erected a working replica of Mount Vesuvius that spewed smoke. Genovese fashioned his estate after those he was familiar with in Nola, near Naples, Italy, where he was born.

Although these were the Depression years, Genovese spared no expense. Many of the rare plants he placed here can still be seen, including the unique Sargent's weeping hemlock—said to be the largest on the east coast—which forms an umbrella over three cascading pools.

In 1937, when Thomas E. Dewey, then a special prosecutor, began singling Genovese out as an organized-crime boss, the family quickly fled to Europe. Genovese sold the property for $35,000 to Mary Gladys Cubbage of Rumson in 1948, and it was sold again to Karl and Marjorie Wihtol four years before Genovese was finally sentenced in this country on narcotics charges. The Wihtols built the present house, which now serves as the visitors center, and expanded the gardens and greenhouses surrounding the house to form a living catalog of plants.

Stroll down the path to the hillside gardens, which contain a large variety of exotic trees. The 11-foot Alberta spruce and the Sargent's weeping hemlock, measuring 35 feet across, are particularly impressive. Eventually the beautiful walkways will bring you to the meadow, where the swimming pool Genovese had built now lies buried. Nearby is his pergola, covered with magnificent kiwi and clematis vines. A tiny brook runs along this garden, a paradise for white-throated sparrows, titmice, quail, cardinals, chickadees, and downy woodpeckers.

Each spring, Deep Cut Gardens—named for the stream that trickles down into a narrow gorge—sports huge displays of nodding daffodils at the entrance to the gardens and along the path leading to the gazebo near lush evergreens. It is during this time that the magnolias burst open with white blossoms, and showy columbines line the azalea walk. Here, too, thousands of tulips poke their way up through the ground.

Don't leave without going into the greenhouse to see the collection of succulents Mrs. Wihtol brought home from her travels throughout the United States, South America, and South Africa, as well as the large collection of orchids.

The property Genovese loved so much was in ruins when he sold it to Mary Gladys Cubbage, but it was lovingly restored by the Wihtols, who willed half of it to Monmouth County with the provision that they purchase the rest. When the county park system took over in 1977, the house was converted to classrooms, a garden gift shop, a library, and offices.

NOTE: The Elvin McDonald Horticultural Library (open during park hours), located in the main building and reputed to be one of the largest horticultural libraries on the east coast, has 3,000 books and catalogs available for instant reference. Pack a picnic lunch and enjoy it on one of the benches in the rockery, the front gardens, one of the picnic tables near the parking lot, or in the park opposite Deep Cut Gardens.

67
Holmes-Hendrickson Kitchen Garden

LOCATION ❧ Monmouth County
Longstreet and Roberts Roads
Holmdel 07733
732-462-1466

GARDEN SIZE ❧ Less than ¼ acre

ADMISSION ❧ *Garden:* No charge. *House:* Fee.

WHEN TO VISIT ❧ *Garden:* Dawn to dusk daily, May through
September. *House:* May through September,
Tuesday, Thursday, and Sunday 1–4; Saturday
10–4.

HIGHLIGHTS ❧ Authentic Colonial herb garden and mid-18th-
century farmhouse

FACILITIES ❧ None

EVENTS ❧ Wool Day celebration and spinning wheel exhibit
each April. Call for a schedule.

According to New Jersey landscape architect Frederick C. Kniesler Jr., Colonial gardens evolved as need arose within a particular household and as the housewife's preferences changed. Seeds and slips of plants brought from abroad were supplemented by native plants found in local fields, forests, and by trading with neighbors. Colonial gardens were located outside the kitchen for convenience rather than fashion, were often weedy, and in addition to an abundance of herbs grown for seasoning food, contained a variety of flowers that could be dried for winter use, decorations, and potpourri. These gardens, according to Kniesler, differed depending on the homeowner's nationality. "Dutch settlers used a lot of flowering bulbs; Spaniards incorporated orchards; while the English used a lot of flowers within ordered beds."

The Kitchen Garden adjacent to the Holmes-Hendrickson House is a fine example of what American housewives planted outside the kitchen door in 1790. The striking mix of flowers, herbs, and vegetables in this tiny but elegant garden were chosen according to original notes and sources dating to the Colonial period. For example, lemon-yellow daylilies, rather than today's usual orange variety, were planted, and red and blue phlox rather than the modern variegated type. It was also common to place colorful flowering shrubs at key locations where they could be admired. Lilacs were often planted near the dining room area for their beauty as well as their wonderful fragrance.

Among the herbs represented is catnip, used in making tea and cat toys; sweet basil, favored as a seasoning; red bay, for adding flavor to meats and sweets and as a scent for clothes and finger bowls; and chives, grown as a seasoning all year long. Flowers, which often provided the only color in an otherwise drab household, include hollyhock and hydrangea, often dried for special arrangements; foxgloves, used for medicinal purposes; and nasturtiums, for its edible leaves and seeds. The Johnny-jump-ups had multiple uses: Its flowers were dried for potpourri, used in perfumes, or dropped into warm water for a soothing bath; the leaves were added to salads; and the flowers were a favorite candied confection. There's lots more planted in this kitchen garden, including tansy, yarrow, primrose, lavender, and thyme.

Follow the brick walk to the Holmes-Hendrickson House, a mid-18th-century house restored by the Monmouth County Historical Association. Designed to resemble an English-style Georgian house from the outside, the inside construction and interior arrangement of the rooms reflect the Dutch heritage of its builder. Now operated as a museum, the house is interpreted to the latter part of the 18th century when Garret Hendrickson farmed here.

68
Holmdel Arboretum

LOCATION ❧ Monmouth County
Holmdel Park
Longstreet Road
Holmdel Township 07733
732-842-4000
GARDEN SIZE ❧ 20 acres
ADMISSION ❧ No charge
WHEN TO VISIT ❧ 8 AM–dusk daily, year-round
HIGHLIGHTS ❧ Hundreds of species, cultivars, and varieties of
ornamental trees and shrubs
FACILITIES ❧ Rest room, water, refreshment area; picnic tables
and grills inside the 375-acre park

Established in 1963, Holmdel Arboretum's educational and horticultural display is devoted to the culture and study of the trees, shrubs, and other woody plants that grow in the Monmouth County area. Thanks to numerous contributions from local nurserymen, Friends of the Shade Tree Commission, and individuals who have donated in memory of a loved one or friend, the arboretum contains thousands of plants.

Most plantings, divided into sections according to color of bloom, are tagged. Bordering both sides of the pond is the red section where each spring the crab apple, hawthorn, and cherry collections bloom in every shade of red imaginable.

The Jane Kluis Memorial Dwarf Conifer Garden, donated by nurseryman Rudy Kluis in memory of his wife, has a bluish tone, providing an especially attractive contrast against the larger evergreens and deciduous plants. The Pine and Cedar Collection, donated in memory of David Rossheim, is in the dark-green area, while the Alvarez Synoptic Garden, donated by Alberto Alvarez in 1977, consists of shrubs and trees planted in alphabetical order.

Holmdel Arboretum contains thousands of trees, shrubs, and plants.

Ground covers add to the all-around splendor of this arboretum, as well as the abundant juniper, cotoneaster, and holly—all maintained by the Monmouth County Shade Tree Commission in cooperation with the Monmouth County Park System.

NOTE: Adjacent to the arboretum are nature trails leading through mature stands of American beech; white, red, and chestnut oaks; and hickory. The park is also the site of Longstreet Farm, a 300-year-old farm restored to the period 1890–1900, with original farm machinery, tools, and implements demonstrated by park system farmers dressed in period costume.

69

Lambertus C. Bobbink Memorial Rose Garden in Thompson Park

LOCATION ❧ Monmouth County
805 Newman Springs Road (Route 520)
Thompson Park
Lincroft 07738
732-842-4000

GARDEN SIZE ❧ Less than ½ acre

ADMISSION ❧ No charge

WHEN TO VISIT ❧ Daily 8 AM to dusk, year-round. Peak bloom is in June and July.

HIGHLIGHTS ❧ Prizewinning roses; gazebo; beautiful fountain

FACILITIES ❧ Rest room

EVENTS ❧ Pony and wagon rides, children's races, an arts and crafts sale, demonstrations, and outdoor entertainment throughout the year. Write or call for a schedule.

Philanthropist and social activist Geraldine Thompson was generous throughout her lifetime, so it isn't surprising that in 1968 she bequeathed Brookdale Farm, her 215-acre estate, to the citizens of Monmouth County. This land became the nucleus for Thompson Park; with the addition of surrounding property, the park has increased to 665 acres.

Thanks to the generosity of Dorothea Bobbink White and her husband, George White, area residents benefit from another gift: a rose garden. On her way home from an All-America Rose Selections (AARS) Awards luncheon in 1972, Ms. White decided to honor her late father, Lambertus C. Bobbink, by building a rose garden in his name. It was an ideal memorial for him. His nursery, the Bobbink and Atkins Nursery, had gained national attention, and he was known worldwide as "The Dean of Commercial Rosarians in America." The Monmouth County Parks Department agreed, and selected a site next to the former Thompson Mansion, which is also headquarters for the Monmouth County Parks System. Demitry Levitsky, the park's landscape architect, drafted the site plan.

Before construction of the garden even began, the Public Gardens Committee of the AARS appointed the Thompson Park locale an official AARS public rose garden as well as a demonstration garden, where new rose varieties would be planted for an entire season before going on the market to see how they fare. Those designated as AARS trial roses would be planted in a nearby area to be judged by a demonstration garden supervisor.

The garden was dedicated in 1977. Visitors strolling through this exquisite, well-maintained garden—tended single-handedly by park naturalist Steve Dickinson—can enjoy the original roses as well as many new varieties. A gazebo and fountain were also given to the garden by the Whites "for the enjoyment of all those who love roses," as the memorial plaque at the garden's entrance denotes.

Each bush is tagged with the name and year the specific variety was selected for the AARS award, and while peak bloom is during June, July, and August, there's always something in bloom from May through October. You'll find oldies here including a 1949 'White Dawn', a climber lavish with huge blooms during spring and autumn; a 1955 'Tiffany' hybrid tea rose, with large pink blossoms and a fruity fragrance; the 1986 'Voodoo', a heavily perfumed hybrid tea that comes in a multitude of colors; and the 1996 'St. Patrick' hybrid tea, a stunning yellow flower showing a hint of green.

The Visitors Center is housed in the former mansion built by William Payne Thompson in 1893. The building's three floors and basement originally included 32 rooms, 13 bathrooms, and 16 fireplaces. According to park officials, Geraldine Thompson and her husband, Lewis, were the mansion's last occupants, having raised four children of their own and five orphaned children of relatives there. After Lewis Thompson died in 1936, his wife carried on the family's lifelong tradition of generosity, one that lives on in this park even after her death in 1967 at the age of 95.

70
Allen House Herb Garden

LOCATION ❧ Monmouth County
Route 35 and Sycamore Avenue
Shrewsbury 07702
732-462-1466
GARDEN SIZE ❧ Less than ¼ acre
ADMISSION ❧ *Garden:* No charge. *House:* Fee.
WHEN TO VISIT ❧ *Garden:* Dawn to dusk daily, May through
September. *House:* May through September,
Tuesday, Thursday, and Sunday 1–4, Saturday
10–4.
HIGHLIGHTS ❧ Colonial herb garden and circa-1688 house
FACILITIES ❧ Rest room when house is open
EVENTS ❧ Changing exhibits in the Allen House. Call for
schedule.

This lovely, well-maintained herb garden was designed and planted by the Shrewsbury Garden Club in 1974.

The herbs in this garden were chosen to represent plantings typical of the 18th century. Each served a specific purpose, whether for flavoring food, supplying medicines, dyeing linens or yarns, repelling insects, attracting bees, or providing color indoors at weddings or baptisms.

Follow the brick path from the parking area to the garden to see and smell this wonderful array of herbs, all of which are labeled with their common and Latin names. You'll find nutmeg thyme, mother-of-thyme, dill, winter savory, sweet marjoram, chives, foxglove, and oregano, plus an Egyptian top onion sporting a weird-shaped onion growing on top of the plant. You'll also find a fine collection of oregano, borage, lavender, germander, santolina, horehound, hyssop, chamomile, rue, rosemary, white yarrow, thistle, lemon balm, French tarragon, sage, and bedstraw. This last was specifically grown in Colonial times for use in stuffing mattresses because it was bug-free.

After you've seen the garden, take a tour of Allen House, a handsome structure that served through the years as a private residence, a meeting room during the Revolutionary period, a tavern, a tearoom, and an antiques shop. Following its acquisition by the Monmouth County Historical Association in 1968, the house was restored as an excellent example of an 18th-century tavern. Built in 1688 by Judah Allen, a Quaker settler, Allen House was sold to Josiah Halstead in 1764. Realizing the property was located along a popular carriage stop, Halstead enlarged the house so he could turn it into a tavern and inn for weary travelers. According to the historical association, "Halstead's house served as a court, town hall, post office, dance hall, and simply a gathering place for the people of Shrewsbury. Surviving documents, such as tavern keepers' accounts, town record books, notices for meetings, court records, and travelers' accounts offer glimpses of the many activities that took place at Halstead's tavern and similar establishments throughout 18th-century New Jersey."

71

St. Mary's Roman Catholic Church Butterfly Garden

LOCATION 🌺	Mercer County
	Highway 34 and Phalanx Road
	Colts Neck 07722
	732-780-2666
GARDEN SIZE 🌺	Less than ¼ acre
ADMISSION 🌺	No charge
WHEN TO VISIT 🌺	Dawn to dusk daily, year-round
HIGHLIGHTS 🌺	Lovely grounds, bell tower, grotto
FACILITIES 🌺	Rest rooms when the church is open.
EVENTS 🌺	Celebration Mass at the grotto during May. Call for date.

According to Jeffrey Glassberg, approximately 3,000 people have joined the North American Butterfly Association since he founded the organization in Morristown, New Jersey, in 1993. There are hundreds of thousands of additional fans throughout the United States who spend their leisure time watching these beautiful invertebrates.

Visitors can see dozens of these dazzling symbols of hope and renewal hovering over the flowers in this tiny, exquisite garden planted by members of the R.F.D. Garden Club in 1993. According to member Marie Savoia, the club—named for the rural free-delivery post office it meets in—refurbished an old garden on the church grounds in preparation for a flower show the club held in September 1993. After undesirable plants were removed, the shrubs and trees were pruned, and butterfly-friendly plants placed in the garden. The garden was so successful at attracting butterflies that members decided to continue maintaining the garden after the show was over. The garden is now tended by members of the Environmental Committee of St. Mary's Church.

St. Mary's Roman Catholic Church Butterfly Garden

Each summer a kaleidoscope of flowers stands out spectacularly against a backdrop of deep-green trees and shrubbery. Holly, purple coneflower, Nanho blue buddleia, and butterfly-blue scabiosa are planted around the perimeter, while annuals are tucked between huge boulders scattered throughout the garden area. Butterfly-friendly perennial beds include lavender, yarrow, butterfly weed, helianthus, New England aster, and goldenrod, while zinnia, tithonia, globe amaranth, lantana, dwarf marigold, and cosmos comprise the annual plantings. Various sages and a grouping of hyssop and catnip make a nice showing, as does the 'Autumn Joy' sedum.

The rest of the grounds are landscaped with cherry trees and a variety of pines. Finally, don't miss the grotto hugging the hillside a short distance from the garden. Inspired by a grotto at Notre Dame, each year it is planted with hundreds of annuals. The grotto—surrounded by low juniper, hybrid rhododendrons, azalea, forsythia, and holly, along with linden, dogwood, maple, crab apple, and pine trees—is a beautiful place to meditate as well as a great vantage point from which to admire the well-kept grounds. It is here that Father Edward Griswold, the current pastor, conducts a service honoring the Blessed Mother each May.

A profusion of hydrangeas surrounds the fountain at Veterans Park Gardens.

72

Veterans Park Gardens

LOCATION ❧ Mercer County
2206 Kuser Road
Hamilton 08690
609-581-4124

GARDEN SIZE ❧ Approximately 1½ acres within the 329-acre park

ADMISSION ❧ No charge

WHEN TO VISIT ❧ Dawn to dusk daily, year-round

HIGHLIGHTS ❧ Outstanding hydrangeas, perennials, and annuals surrounding a fountain in the formal garden.

FACILITIES ❧ Rest room, water, benches

This pleasant formal garden, located within Veterans Park, is the perfect place to get away from everyday stresses. Choose any bench facing the fountain in the center of a 30-foot pool, and listen to the falling water while surrounded by beautiful flowers, shrubs, and trees. During spring, daffodils and tulips pop up everywhere in this area, followed by colorful impatiens, salvia, canna lilies, foxgloves, and annual plantings of begonias in the circular beds surrounding the pool.

Many beautiful shrubs also grow in the formal garden, including azaleas, adorned with pink and white blossoms in spring; viburnums, easily identified by their opposing leaves and blossoms arranged in umbrella-shaped clusters; and massive Peegee hydrangeas, bearing huge snowball-sized blossoms. Each fall, brightly colored chrysanthemums highlight the area beneath tall pines, oaks, and the Yoshino and 'Kwanzan' cherry trees.

After admiring this attractive, well-maintained formal garden, stretch your legs along the 2½-mile path that winds through the 329-acre park—the first in the state to receive a Green Acres grant, a 50–50 matching grant between the state and the township, in 1966. Fifty years ago, all that was here was farmland. Thanks to additional funding received from the town, after the park was completed in 1981, hundreds of wildflowers, azaleas, and rhododendrons were planted in the natural areas. A bog garden can be reached via a boardwalk.

Thanks to a program that started here in 1982, individuals can donate trees in honor of a loved one. The first 12 trees from this program were planted on the east side of the park. However, the response was so overwhelming that planting quickly expanded to other areas. To date, over 200 trees have been donated, including red, scarlet, and pin oaks; red, sugar, and 'Crimson King' maples; dogwoods; and cherries.

NOTE: The John Abbott House (open weekends and Christmas); an original barn from the late 1700s, and the Civil War Museum (open weekends) is located at the park's south side, which is also extensively planted with flower beds and specimen trees. There are tennis courts and ball fields on the park's south side. Park events include Septemberfest and a Civil War Reenactment in August; call for dates and times.

73
Sayen Gardens

LOCATION ❧ Mercer County
155 Hughes Drive
Hamilton 08650
609-890-3543 or 609-890-3874

GARDEN SIZE ❧ Approximately 30 acres

ADMISSION ❧ No charge

WHEN TO VISIT ❧ Dawn to dusk daily, year-round

HIGHLIGHTS ❧ Magnificent azalea and rhododendron displays

FACILITIES ❧ Rest room; handicapped-accessible

EVENTS ❧ Azalea Festival and house tours on Mother's Day weekend; ecology programs for Scouts, schools, and garden clubs

Fred Sayen made many trips to China, Japan, and England, and amassed a huge collection of azaleas and rhododendrons. In order to continue his favorite hobby—gardening—in 1912, for one dollar, he purchased this 30-acre site to house his plants. Today, about 2,000 azaleas and 1,500 rhododendrons still thrive where he planted them, in addition to the many dogwoods, redbuds, magnolias, and evergreens he added through the years.

According to Supervising Horticulturist Harry Robinson, many new garden areas have been planted since Sayen's death, and he notes, "they're maintained according to Sayen's original plan of natural landscaping. One of the additions is a beautiful pond. It's stocked with comets and shebunkins and heavily planted with marginals and water lilies. There's also a pretty bridge over the pond, a beautiful wooden gazebo, plaza fountain, marble temple, large trellises with vines, and plenty of benches and seating areas."

Bloom at Sayen Gardens begins toward the end of February and continues until Christmas. Spring is the start of a spectacular display of approximately 500,000 daffodils, tulips, snowdrops, and various other bulbs. The inviting path that winds through the entire garden area is handicapped-accessible, and the short, easy woodland walk is refreshing—especially on a hot summer day when a green canopy provides natural shade.

An avid gardener, Sayen—who owned one of the earliest industries in Hamilton, the successful Mercer Rubber Company—thoroughly landscaped the area around his house and planted many exotic plants gathered from the countries he visited, rising early each morning to spend time in the garden. As he grew older and gardening became more difficult, he subdivided and sold quite a bit of his property, donating to the township a large plot of land where the Nottingham Little League is now situated. After his death in 1981 at the age of 97, the township, encouraged by Mayor John K. Rafferty, purchased the property from the Sayen family and opened it to the public in 1988. It is maintained by the Hamilton Township Grounds Keepers.

On Mother's Day, Sayen's unusual 17-room bungalow-style house is open for tours. Sayen and his wife, Anne Mellon, drew inspiration for their arts and crafts–influenced house from the work of the Greene Brothers of Southern California. The interior displays a strong Victorian influence with heavily draped windows and dark paneling.

NOTE: The house can be rented for weddings and parties.

Dimitri Hadzi's sculpture Centaur *was placed at Prospect Gardens in Princeton in honor of Robert F. Goheen, the president of Princeton University from 1957 to 1972.*

"A Mother's Garden," one of two lovely pocket-sized gardens at the Clinton Historical Museum Gardens, faces the Hunterdon Museum of Art.

The Lambertus C. Bobbink Memorial Rose Garden in Thompson Park is an All-America Rose Selection trial and demonstration garden.

Sixty-year-old Chinese wisteria embrace the Doric columns at Van Vleck Gardens in Montclair.

A tiger swallowtail visits the flowers at St. Mary's Roman Catholic Church Butterfly Garden in Colts Neck.

Over 1,500 tulips bloom each spring at Port Imperial Gardens in Weehawken.

In April the Japanese cherry trees burst into bloom at Warinanco Park Gardens in Roselle.

Earth Mother,
a 1986 bronze
sculpture by
Allan Houser,
graces the
grounds of the
Van Vleck
Arboretum at the
Montclair Art
Museum.

Eolith, carved from Blue Mountain granite by New Jersey sculptor Isaac Witkin, can be seen at Grounds for Sculpture, located on the former New Jersey State Fairgrounds in Hamilton.

Columbines entice butterflies at the Karl Ninnemann, Jr. Memorial Butterfly Garden at Island Beach State Park.

In spring the crabapples, hawthorns, and cherries at Holmdel Arboretum bloom in a spectrum of pinks and reds.

A medieval-style birdhouse, built especially for doves, adorns the cottage garden at Atlock Farm Garden in Somerset.

Coleus and impatiens nestle among the rocks at Sayen Gardens in Hamilton.

The Mercer Oak at Princeton Battlefield State Park was just a sapling when General Hugh Mercer fell nearby during the Battle of Princeton on January 3, 1777.

Hostas encircle a wooded glade at Quietude Sculpture Garden in East Brunswick.

The tranquil half-acre Edith Duff Gwinn Gardens are tended by the Garden Club of Long Beach Island and the Barnegat Light Historical Society.

A visitor admires the Donald B. Lacey Annual Display Garden at the Rutgers Display Gardens in New Brunswick.

74
Grounds For Sculpture

LOCATION ❧ Mercer County
18 Fairgrounds Road
Hamilton 08619
609-586-0616
Web site: www.groundsforsculpture.org

GARDEN SIZE ❧ 22 acres

ADMISSION ❧ No charge

WHEN TO VISIT ❧ Friday through Sunday 10–4, year-round, or by appointment Tuesday through Thursday, 9–4. Closed Monday and major holidays. Peak bloom for crocuses, daffodils, forsythias, crab apples, and dogwoods is early spring; May and June are peak bloom for pears, redbuds, azaleas, rhododendrons, daylilies, virburnums, and roses.

HIGHLIGHTS ❧ Outdoor sculpture installations sited in a gently rolling terrain with open spaces, courtyards, gardens, and pools. Various ecosystems containing over 1,000 trees of more than 100 varieties; flowers and ornamental grasses; two glass-walled museum buildings featuring contemporary monumental and smaller scale works by American and internationally known artists.

FACILITIES ❧ Rest room, water, restaurant, alfresco café, and museum shop. Partially handicapped-accessible grounds and Museum Building; fully accessible Domestic Arts Building. Pets are not allowed

EVENTS ❧ Regularly scheduled exhibitions. Call for schedule.

From 1888, this was the home of the Inter-State Fair, later renamed the New Jersey State Fair. The fair site sat idle from 1980 to 1987, until J. Seward Johnson Jr. decided to transform the grounds and buildings into a public sculpture garden and museum that would be adjacent to the Johnson Atelier Technical Institute of Sculpture. Johnson, a world-famous sculptor, founded the Atelier in 1974 as a school for those who wanted to learn about casting and the specialized workings of an art foundry.

Johnson's dream was to make sculpture accessible to everyone and to help people become more comfortable with art. To realize his dream, Johnson purchased the vacant land, and in 1989 began the renovation with architectural plans and landscape design executed by Brian Carey of AC/BC Associates of New York City. Extensive plantings of more than 500 trees and thousands of rose bushes, flowers, and shrubs were brought in to turn the previously desolate site into a showplace. The landscaped hills, valleys, islands of trees, berms, waterways, courtyards, and a pond provide striking backdrops for the plants and sculptures contained on these exceptionally beautiful 22 acres.

After parking and entering the huge steel-frame structure that now serves as an indoor museum, be sure to obtain a free map of the grounds. But before setting foot outside, spend some time inside this two-story recycled structure. When the fairgrounds were still in operation, this building was used to display farm animals. Fortunately it was saved, and the renovation features vast glass walls. Now this former industrial space is a light and airy museum whose spacious dimensions provide ample room for exhibitions and give visitors the illusion of being out-doors. Three of the original 37-foot-high steel arches have been moved outside, where they now serve as a vine-covered arbor. Then head over to the Domestic Arts Building, formerly the New Jersey State Fair exhibit hall. Opened in May 1997, it provides an additional 10,000 square feet of indoor exhibition space for sculpture.

Since its opening in 1992, Grounds For Sculpture has attracted thousands of visitors year-round. New sculptures are always being added; indoor exhibitions change frequently, and one can never tire of the huge variety of plants. Spring, when the Kousa dogwood, Cornelian cherry dogwood, weeping forsythia, mountain laurel, rhododendron, crab apple, Japanese cherry, 'Shubert' cherry, and Japanese and Chinese wisteria are in bloom, is especially lovely. Hundreds of daffodils also make an appearance this time of year.

As you stroll over the gently rolling, well-manicured terrain, you'll find more than 100 works of sculpture. The park hosts continuous exhibitions of works by internationally known artists—including Isaac Witkin, Anthony Caro, and Beverly Pepper—in many different media, including metal, wood, concrete, and stone. One of my favorite pieces is near the lake, but you'll have to really search for it, even when armed with a map. When Johnson executed this multifigure bronze work entitled *Déjeuner Déjà Vu* in 1994, inspired by Manet's provocative painting *Déjeuner sur l'Herbe*, he had the earth raised behind a manufactured waterfall and enclosed the sculpture within a circle of trees and bushes. He left only one narrow opening because "Having that one viewing spot from Manet's perspective is like peeking, so to speak, into the painting." Entering this eerie space never fails to surprise visitors.

In the short time that Grounds For Sculpture has been in existence, it has succeeded in accomplishing its mission to "exhibit, interpret, and promote contemporary sculpture." It has also succeeded in creating various types of ecosystems, including woods, marshes, meadows, and ponds, that are rich in natural beauty and worth a repeat visit.

NOTE: Combine a visit to the Grounds For Sculpture with a tour of the adjacent Johnson Atelier, one of the world's leading fine art foundries. There you'll learn, and see, how sculptors work. Tours (by appointment only; 15 years and over; fee; call 609-890-7777) take about an hour.

75
William Trent House Garden

LOCATION ❧ Mercer County
15 Market Street
Trenton 08611
609-989-3027

GARDEN SIZE ❧ Less than 2 acres

ADMISSION ❧ *Garden:* No charge. *House tour:* Fee.

WHEN TO VISIT ❧ Daily 12:30–4, year-round; closed major holidays

HIGHLIGHTS ❧ A peaceful Colonial garden divided into several areas of interest; Trent House, an 18th-century summer home with fine examples of William and Mary furniture

FACILITIES ❧ Rest room inside house when museum is open; water fountain along the north wall of the Carriage House

EVENTS ❧ Holiday Open House in December; lectures and programs throughout the year. Call for schedule.

A visit to the Trent House is, according to the brochure, a "step back in time to 1719—before George Washington was born, before the Revolution had been thought of." It is, indeed, for today the house and garden William Trent built as his summer residence look much the way they did in Colonial times. The only difference is that this entire area was a wilderness when Trent had purchased the property.

Born in Scotland, by 1682 Trent had grown rich as a merchant trader and shipbuilder in Philadelphia. Tax records indicate that his business thrived: He exported tobacco, flour, skins, and furs, and imported wine, rum, molasses, and dry goods, as well as slaves from Africa and indentured servants from the British Isles. Like other gentlemen of his wealth and stature, Trent built this fine Georgian mansion in New Jersey at the falls of the Delaware far away from the dirt and bustle of the city. It served as a summer residence for Trent, his second wife, Mary Coddington, their young son, William Jr., and 11 African slaves who ran the country house as well as several mills he constructed along the Assunpink Creek. Eventually, Trent laid out streets and city lots, and named the area Trent's Town.

The property changed hands frequently after his death in 1724, until Edward Ansley Stokes, the last owner, presented the City of Trenton with the mansion in 1929 on the condition that it be restored to its original state and used as an art gallery, library, or historical museum. When the trustees of the library received the property from the city, they chose to preserve it as an early American home; furnishings were selected to correspond with inventoried items that were in the house under Trent's ownership.

The house has been beautifully restored, and during the 1-hour daily tour you'll learn how this wealthy family lived. You'll also be in for a treat strolling through the beautiful garden that the Garden Club of Trenton designed as a historic re-creation in 1938. Although it isn't an exact replica of the Trent's original garden, it accurately reflects the style of early Colonial gardens. Trent hired landscape architect Isabella Pendletown Bowen to prepare plans according to various written references to the original garden. It contained many ancient specimen trees and was enclosed with a lovely Georgian-style brick wall that still stands. When the restoration was completed, the house was again turned over to the City of Trenton—now responsible for its upkeep— while members of the Garden Club of Trenton care for the garden.

On the garden's north side is a circle of boxwood following the lines of a design noted on a 1789 map of the house and its surroundings. Nearby there's a huge, ancient copper beech, as well as a wall of hemlocks. Three very old box trees front the main entrance of the building on the south. There, a circular brick walk around the center box tree brings visitors to a shaded 18th century–style garden bench, where they can admire the fine Georgian symmetry of the Trent House. During spring, this area is aglow with irises, bleeding hearts, roses, phlox, and lilacs.

Toward the east, English boxwood shrubs mark each corner of the house, and the lawn is bordered by an allée of pear trees that bear ample fruit in the fall. The herb garden, in the western section, was redesigned in 1975 as a simple placement of herbs inside a rectangular box hedge broken into four quadrants. Arranged around a center sundial surrounded by English, creeping, golden, woolly, and variegated thyme, the garden's quadrants are planted by type of herb: namely culinary, medicinal, ornamental, and potpourri. Through the iron gates in the west wall, visitors can relax at picnic tables in a grove of trees. From this area, you can see the old carriage house, now used as the caretaker's residence.

Before leaving, consider signing up for a tour of the mansion. There you'll see a few of the family's prized possessions, including a tea set with porcelain teacups imported from China, an Elizabethan game box dating from the first half of the 17th century, and an unusual circa-1690 English daybed, an excellent example of made-to-order furniture from that era.

NOTE: Parking is free in the state parking lot just beyond the Trent House grounds.

Southern
New Jersey

76

S. Mary Grace Burns Arboretum

LOCATION ❦ Ocean County
Georgian Court College
900 Lakewood Avenue
Lakewood 08701
732-364-2200

GARDEN SIZE ❦ 152 acres

ADMISSION ❦ Fee for self-guiding arboretum brochure required;
available at the college library

WHEN TO VISIT ❦ Dawn to dusk, Monday through Friday, year-round

HIGHLIGHTS ❦ Native and exotic tree species; vast plantings of
annuals and perennials; plus grounds resembling a
Georgian period English estate

FACILITIES ❦ Rest room, cafeteria, handicapped-accessible

EVENTS ❦ Hour-long garden tours, for adults only, are
scheduled for groups of 15 or more persons for a
small fee. Call 732-364-2200 ext. 266 for
information.

In 1896, George Jay Gould—millionaire son of railroad tycoon Jay Gould—purchased this 150-acre property for his winter residence. Bruce Price, a famous New York architect, was hired to design the grounds in the style of a Georgian-period English estate, and to create three major gardens that would blend in with the natural surroundings. After Gould died in 1923, his heirs sold the property to the Sisters of Mercy of North Plainfield, New Jersey, with the stipulation that the name of the estate, Georgian Court, be retained. The following year, the Sisters opened Georgian Court College, a Catholic liberal arts college and graduate

One of the many garden areas at S. Mary Grace Burns Arboretum

school, open to students of all faiths. The estate is now designated a National Historic Site, and is a recognized National Landmark and National Arboretum.

The Classic Garden, inspired by the formal gardens of Italy, features life-sized statues of Greek gods and goddesses and figures representing the seasons. Floral urns grace the garden, and semicircular pergolas are near the Casino building. Built in 1899 for indoor recreation during inclement weather, the Casino contains a bowling alley, racquetball court, tennis court, squash court, billiard room, and a swimming pool.

An impressive Himalayan pine, characterized by its long needles in bunches of five, grows on the vast lawn near the Farley Memorial Library. Near the Arts and Science Center, the main academic building on campus, stands a tall Norway spruce with slender, needlelike, four-sided leaves; and an old European beech, identified by its smooth gray bark and bright yellow leaves in autumn. Horse chestnuts line both sides of the exit road, while closer to the Science Center are a number of oaks, many bearing lightning scars.

It's easy to spot the huge 200-year-old white oak, for it stands majestically in a large field adjacent to the Science Center. American basswood trees, also known as lindens, can be found along the road behind the Casino. Here, too, are chestnut oaks, Norway spruces, and to the left of the lion sculpture along the concrete path, a large Oriental spruce with short needles. Nearby, there's also a moss cypress, a Norway spruce, and a pitch pine.

The exquisite Japanese Garden is entered through a gateway called a *machiai*. Follow the path to the genuine teahouse, and cross over the small wooden footbridge to see trees, including black oak, Colorado blue spruce, Japanese maple, and Japanese cherry. Birds seem to congregate at this peaceful garden, especially around the beautiful Chinese juniper, Japanese yews, and several weeping Higan cherry trees.

A short distance away is Founder's Grove. Established by four research students and their mentor, it contains a Chinese scholar tree, a Serbian spruce, a Japanese white pine, a weeping Norway spruce, and a dawn redwood. Nearby you'll find the Fountain of Apollo, a birthday gift Gould presented to his wife in 1902. Water for the fountain, drawn from Lake Carasaljo, is turned on for special occasions. The figure of Apollo drives a chariot drawn by rearing horses; the elaborate sculpture also includes sea horses, cherubs, and fish.

Four 8-foot marble urns and moss cypresses flank either side of the road on the approach to the Sunken Garden, which is connected via a lagoon to Lake Carasaljo. Considered the most lavish garden on the estate, its first level contains a 17th-century marble fountain brought here from the South of France. The lower lagoon level features lion sculptures, a continuing theme throughout the estate.

The 50-room mansion, now home for several Sisters of Mercy, features wrought-iron balconies and terra-cotta; windows and doorways accented with white wood and white marble trim; a high French-style roof with pedimented dormers; and tall brick chimneys. The spacious veranda on the south side overlooks a broad lawn and Lake Carasaljo.

A European beech and a white ash are visible as you face the Formal Garden, an elliptical flower garden planted with boxwood hedges that define the mazelike walkways. In the center is a bronze sculpture of three satyrs holding a sundial. Eventually you'll reach Raymond Hall, once part of Gould's stable complex, which was modeled on those Gould had visited in England. Coaches and carriages were housed in the upper portion of this building and were brought down by elevator as needed.

When you come to Mercedes Hall, look for the small rock garden in the center of the circle; it's filled with a variety of flowers and a tall Norway spruce, identified by sharp-tipped dark green needles. Here you'll find winged euonymus, flowering dogwood, and unusual trees, including a weeping birch, white mulberry, Dunstan hybrids of the American chestnut, and an Atlas blue cedar. A memorial to Sister Mary Grace Burns, the first chairperson of the biology department, stands here as a tribute to the many hours she spent planting, maintaining, and identifying the trees on this magnificent campus.

77

Sambol-Citta Arboretum

LOCATION ❧ Ocean County
Ocean County College
College Drive
Toms River 08753
732-255-4000

GARDEN SIZE ❧ 10 acres

ADMISSION ❧ No charge

WHEN TO VISIT ❧ Dawn to dusk daily, year-round

HIGHLIGHTS ❧ Nearly every tree and shrub native to New Jersey

FACILITIES ❧ Benches

A bronze plaque at the entrance to Sambol-Citta Arboretum (directly across from the main entrance of Ocean County College) reads, "Its purpose is to provide a retreat of repose and natural beauty for the human, a refuge for the birds and a place for the student of New Jersey plants." Although still in its infancy, since its dedication in 1983 the arboretum has been growing by leaps and bounds and will certainly fulfill its original promise.

Groves of pitch pine, red pine, and white spruce are here. During spring you'll smell the wonderful fragrance of dense clumps of lilacs. In this area, abundant dogwood and mountain laurel make an appearance before you come upon the wide expanse of manicured lawn, which is surrounded by several divided sections. In the Pinetum, you'll find an enormous Norway spruce. The nearby Azalea Grove is wonderful in late April; and in the right quadrant, there are impressive pin oaks, red maples, cherry trees, and silver maples.

The beautiful Holly Grove to the right of the pond is a good spot to photograph the birds that are attracted to its bright berries. Nearby are rhododendrons, sweet gums, silver and red maples, and pin oaks. The ferns in the Fern Cobble are fascinating in spring when their fiddleheads unfurl, and at any time of year the stately copper beech is worth a pause.

Thanks to foundation members Richard S. Sambol and Joseph A. Citta, who initiated the development of the arboretum to stimulate interest in the environmental sciences and to enhance the beauty of the campus, this is definitely a place to come back to if you'd like to be alone and absorb the surroundings in peace and quiet.

NOTE: Plan on stretching your legs along the 1.5-mile nature trail next to the arboretum. The vegetation changes dramatically over this short distance. You'll find pitch pines; a hardwood swamp of red maple, sour gum, and sweet bog magnolia; and a cedar swamp.

78

The Lewis W. Barton Arboretum and Nature Preserve

LOCATION ❧ Burlington County
NJ Route 70
Medford 08055
609-654-3000

GARDEN SIZE ❧ Approximately 160 acres, including landscaped grounds, courtyard gardens, wildflower meadows, and woodlands.

ADMISSION ❧ No charge

WHEN TO VISIT ❧ Monday through Friday 8 AM–dusk; Saturday 9 AM–dusk; year-round. Crocus bloom in March; daffodils and forsythias in April; rhododendrons, Bradford pears, and various fruit trees in May; and June brings abundant roses, magnolias, mountain laurels, and wildflowers. Crape myrtles, Franklin trees, and roses are out in August; pyracanthas are in fruit in September; in addition to the fall foliage, nandinas are in fruit in October.

HIGHLIGHTS ❧ Collections of trees and shrubs from many parts of the world; courtyard gardens; wildflower meadows; natural woodlands and wetlands; plus great bird-watching opportunities

FACILITIES ❧ Rest room; water; partially handicapped-accessible

Although the Medford Leas Retirement Community is a private development, the public is welcome to enjoy its beautifully landscaped

Trout lily at the Lewis W. Barton Arboretum and Nature Preserve

grounds. Here you'll find courtyard gardens, wildflower meadows, natural woodlands and wetlands, a collection of trees and shrubs from many parts of the world, and easy walking trails. All that's required is that you sign in at the office upon arrival. While there, ask for a map of the grounds.

This continuing-care retirement community—which sits on the edge of the New Jersey pine barrens—is named in honor of Lewis W. Barton, an experienced horiculturalist, who had a great appreciation of nature and who helped establish Medford Leas. Spring and fall are particularly lovely in this area, for they are the best seasons to observe a few of the more than 133 bird species that can be seen here.

The Pinetum holds an outstanding collection of evergreens, including exotics like the Bosnian pine, Himalayan pine, Nordman fir, and the Japanese umbrella tree. Special gardens are devoted to rhododendrons, herbs, and to the shrubs and wildflowers commonly found in the nearby pinelands. A grove of conifers indigenous to South Jersey is currently being developed. The Nature Preserve has mature upland oak, beech, and hickory woods, typical of the forest cover once dominant in New Jersey's inner coastal plain, while the flood-plain forest in one section of the preserve features red maple, tulip, ironwood, and sweet gum trees.

Adjacent to the residences are 33 singular courtyard gardens. Each is small but unique, and all can be reached via a covered walkway that makes rainy-day visits possible. Court 2 is beautiful in April, when the grapehollies and magnolias bloom, followed by rhododendrons, azaleas, and leucothoes in May. Court 5 is aglow with myrtle, crab apple, azalea, and Kousa dogwood from late April through May, and tickseed can be seen from June through September. Court 8 features ajuga, lavender, yucca, and sedum during the summer, while Siberian irises and crab apples burst open in May at Court 19, followed by dwarf aster during September and October. Rugosa roses and white lilyturf are abloom into September at Court 29.

If you want to stroll a bit more, try the paved, wheelchair-accessible path starting at the main office. Centurion crab apples grow near the parking lot; along the trail you'll see 'Kwanzan' cherry, white pine, bald cypress, a Kentucky coffee tree, Douglas fir, dogwood, winged sumac, a dawn redwood, winterberry, and many more species. You won't even have to carry a tree identification book, because eye-level tags have been placed in front of each variety. For a longer stretch, try the red trail starting at the woods' edge at the northeast corner of the tennis courts. Along the way, you'll find numerous tagged trees, including black oak, American beech, mockernut hickory, willow oak, river birch, wild cherry, Spanish oak, and white mulberry.

79

The Barclay Farmstead Gardens

LOCATION ❧ Camden County
209 Barclay Lane
Cherry Hill 08002
609-795-6225

GARDEN SIZE ❧ *Herb Garden:* Less than ¼ acre. *Farm Gardens:* 32
acres.

ADMISSION ❧ *Gardens:* No charge. *Barclay Farmhouse:* Fee, except
for Cherry Hill residents.

WHEN TO VISIT ❧ *Garden:* Dawn to dusk daily. *House:* Tuesday
through Friday, 9–4.

HIGHLIGHTS ❧ Historic farmhouse and site, farmstead, apple
orchard, walking trail

FACILITIES ❧ Porta-potty, playground

EVENTS ❧ Changing exhibits throughout the year. Call for
schedule.

The Barclay Homestead, operated by the Township of Cherry Hill
in conjunction with the Friends of Barclay Homestead, stands in the
midst of urban development.

Each spring, the marvelous vista of the restored apple orchard creates a unique reminder of the way this farm must have appeared in the
early 1800s, when South Jersey farmers grew many fine varieties of
apples. Among them was an apple called the Cooper's Russeting, originated by Joseph Cooper, a relative of an early owner of the farmstead.

As one of the first properties settled in this area by Europeans, the
grounds were first occupied by British immigrant John Kay around
1680. Several generations of the Kay family owned the property until
1816, when Joseph Thorn purchased it. It is believed that the present

three-story, 11-room brick farmhouse, now used as a showplace for changing exhibits, various community organizations, and educational purposes, was built by Thorn.

In 1826 the property was sold once again to Joseph Cooper, a sixth generation descendent of the founder of Camden and the owner of Camden's Cooper Ferry, to be used as a summer retreat. Through the years, it was passed down to members of the Cooper family, namely Ellen Cooper Barclay, wife of Charles Barclay; Walter, their son; and Helen, Walter's daughter. In the 1950s, portions of the original farm were sold and turned into the residential community now surrounding the present 32-acre site. The house, occupied by the last Barclay family members until 1929, was purchased, along with the remaining property, in 1974 by the Township of Cherry Hill.

Along the redbrick path to the farmhouse, you'll pass signs detailing the history of Barclay Farmstead. From a distance, you'll see an impressive sycamore and linden near the house, and a small but beautiful herb garden that's outstanding during summer months. It's ringed with marigolds at the border, has coleus and tomatoes in the center, and contains rosemary, bergamot, chives, sedum, rue, tansy, thyme, snapwort, and salad burnet.

From spring through fall you'll find local residents lovingly tending all kinds of flowers, tomatoes, squashes, peppers, morning glories, sunflowers, and other beauties in 16-by-25-foot patches they've rented for the season. If you want to watch what's going on while spotting the profusion of butterflies and birds that visit this peaceful, unusual area, head over to the single bench that's been placed under the shade of a cherry tree.

Before leaving, stretch your legs along the short woodland trail that contains many of the same species present on this land when the Lenni-Lenape Indians farmed it. Farming, milling, and mining transformed this area into the young woodland now before you.

80
The Camden Children's Garden

LOCATION ❧ Camden County
Riverside Drive (on the Delaware River adjacent to Ulysses S. Wiggins Waterfront Park and the New Jersey State Aquarium)
Camden 08103
609-365-5825 or 609-757-7038

GARDEN SIZE ❧ 4 acres

ADMISSION ❧ *Garden:* nominal fee; no charge with admission to the adjacent New Jersey State Aquarium

WHEN TO VISIT ❧ At press time, the garden was scheduled to open summer 1999. Please call before traveling to confirm the schedule and hours of the garden.

HIGHLIGHTS ❧ Hands-on gardens with educational themes

FACILITIES ❧ When the garden is in full operation it will be handicapped-accessible, with rest rooms, water, and an educational center.

EVENTS ❧ Call for a schedule of year-round events.

When completed, the Camden Children's Garden may well be the largest garden of its kind in the nation (as of this writing, the garden is scheduled to open in the summer of 1999). It promises to be a magical place where children and the young at heart can explore and use their imagination while discovering the joys of the natural world.

A variety of year-round themed exhibit gardens will teach children about horticulture. They'll be able to hide in Mr. MacGregor's garden; tell time using their shadows on the sundial; take a whistle-stop train ride on the Garden State Express; and walk through the Jack and the Beanstalk Garden of Giants. They can even climb up a tree fort

210

for a bird's-eye view of the lush green surroundings; feed birds in the wildlife habitat; splash in the bubbling fountains; or observe goldfish swimming in the Water Garden.

Garden themes have been drawn from children's literature, folk tales, local history, and geography. Here, exploring the Secret, Meadow Maze, Dinosaur, Rock, and Butterfly Gardens, adorned with colorful flowers and caterpillar topiary, tiny visitors (and the young at heart) will learn the important role plants play in their daily lives.

The person chiefly responsible for planning this dream garden is Michael Devlin, a lawyer by profession, former councilman, and avid gardener. For years, he generously gave away seeds and flats of new plants grown in his private garden to residents of Camden. He also helped set up a program, known as Grow Lab, in local schools so that children could plant seeds in small pots, nurture them, and eventually transplant and care for the seedlings in their own gardens.

Devlin visualized a large-scale garden where hundreds of children could come to learn more about the world of plants while having fun at the same time. An area adjacent to the New Jersey Aquarium was chosen for its high visibility and potential visitation, with the hope that funds collected from the modest admission fee would help ensure the continued operation of both the garden and the Camden City Garden Club's Community Gardening and Grow Lab programs.

The Camden City Garden Club, Inc., recipient of major honors from President Bush, former New Jersey Governor Kean, and others, is a community-based nonprofit organization responsible for originating the Camden Community Gardening Program in 1985 for the residents of Camden. Today, the club provides county-wide activities to promote community gardening and beautification, conservation of the environment, and prevention of juvenile delinquency, in addition to sponsoring dozens of garden sites and Grow Labs throughout the county.

The Camden Children's Garden project will eventually include a horticultural and environmental education center featuring a greenhouse and classrooms where youth groups, school groups, and families will have a choice of programs.

NOTE: Plan on spending the entire day here; the area and parking lot is police-patrolled. After exploring the garden, check out the exhibits at the adjacent New Jersey State Aquarium; stretch your legs along the mile-long waterfront promenade at Wiggins Waterfront Park; or take the ferry connecting the Camden Waterfront to Penn's Landing in Pennsylvania.

81

Edith Duff Gwinn Gardens of the Barnegat Light Museum

LOCATION ❧ Ocean County
Barnegat Light Museum
Fifth Street and Central Avenue,
Barnegat Light 08006
609-494-3522

GARDEN SIZE ❧ Less than ½ acre

ADMISSION ❧ *Garden:* No charge. *Museum:* Fee.

WHEN TO VISIT ❧ *Garden:* Dawn to dusk daily, year-round. *Museum:* June and September, Saturday and Sunday 2–5; July and August, 2–5 daily.

HIGHLIGHTS ❧ Tranquil setting with plants indigenous to the shore area, adjacent to museum filled with lighthouse memorabilia.

FACILITIES ❧ Rest room and water when museum is open.

I discovered the delightful Edith Duff Gwinn Gardens of the Barnegat Light Museum thanks to a tip from a park ranger stationed at the Barnegat Lighthouse. Only a short drive away, the Gwinn Gardens are located behind the quaint museum building which, until 1951, served as a one-room school. In 1954, both the building and surrounding grounds were turned over to the Borough of Barnegat Light by the Board of Education.

In 1968, the unkempt grounds were transformed into a beautiful garden by Edith Duff Gwinn and Frances Selover. When Ms. Gwinn died, the garden was dedicated in her memory, and continued to be maintained by Ms. Selover until her death in 1993. At that time, members of the Garden Club of Long Beach Island and the Barnegat Light Historical Society took over the responsibility.

Pine-needle paths lead visitors past a wide variety of plants, many native to the area, and to benches and bird baths. Among the many plants found in the herb section are feverfew, used as a headache remedy; sweet woodruff, grown for use in potpourri; lemon balm, prized by the Colonists both medicinally and as a flavoring; and yarrow, used centuries ago by Achilles to stop his comrades' bleeding and grown today for its fine appearance and aroma.

A variety of annuals are planted each year, while the perennials never fail to put on a wonderful show. You'll find the anemone, which according to Greek mythology was formed from Venus's tears as she cried over Adonis's body; the balloon flower, boasting round buds resembling a balloon; and the wallflower, symbol of faithfulness in adversity. Red cedars abound, as do hosta, lilies, ferns, and succulents. If you come during the winter months, you'll find the evergreens are comforting even on the bleakest of days.

Bring a bird identification book, or just sit back and relax on a bench in the circular section of the garden to enjoy the tranquil setting. If the museum is open, stop in and examine the collection of lighthouse memorabilia.

NOTE: The Barnegat Lighthouse is well worth a side trip. Known as Old Barney, the state's best-known landmark provides a magnificent view of Island Beach State Park, Barnegat Bay, and Long Beach Island, if you're willing to climb the 217 steps to the top. (Open weekends in May, September, and October, and every day from Memorial Day through Labor Day, 10–4:30.) Picnic tables are located along Barnegat Inlet and fishing is allowed along the jetty.

The Salem Oak

LOCATION ❧ Salem County
Cemetery at northeast side of West Broadway
Salem

GARDEN SIZE ❧ The oak spans more than ¼ acre

ADMISSION ❧ No charge

WHEN TO VISIT ❧ Year-round. Fall is the most colorful time.

HIGHLIGHTS ❧ The tree, over 500 years old, stands in a historic
cemetery.

FACILITIES ❧ None

In 1887, William Patterson, the first president of the Salem County Historical Society, wrote, "The Friends grave yard in Salem is located on the North East side of West Broadway, opposite Oak Street, and was deeded by Samuel Nicholson and his wife, Ann. Near the entrance gate stands the venerable old white oak that most likely was an attractive young sapling when the first meeting house was staked out."

The mighty oak Patterson described is even more impressive today, and while it's understandable that many of its thick, heavy boughs are supported and strengthened with cables, the sight of this 500-year-old tree, which stands 88 feet high, is unforgettable. During spring, its new leaves unfold, changing from red to pink and finally silvery white, while it sports brilliant reddish-purple foliage in the fall.

Wood from the white oak has always been treasured. Pioneers used its timbers for building their blockhouses, bridges, log cabins, and wine casks, and it was used for building the keel of the frigate *Constitution*, as well as in the keels of the mine sweepers and patrol boats during World War II.

Despite the fact that the official state tree is the red oak, the massive white oak towering over this Quaker cemetery is one of New Jersey's best-known trees. Believed to be the lone survivor of the original forest

The Salem Oak, over 500 years old, towers over the historic cemetery.

that grew here centuries ago, it was beneath its vast canopy that John Fenwick supposedly signed a treaty with the Lenni-Lenape Indians in 1675. Fenwick, a former army major, had left the army seeking peace and adopting the Quaker faith, and after purchasing land in this area from the Indians, named the community Salem, the Hebrew word for peace.

After you've finished admiring this magnificent white oak that stands on the site of the nation's first two Quaker meeting houses, spend some time strolling in the cemetery, where pine, red cedar, Norway spruce, and wild rose and holly shrubs can be seen. Here, according to the Salem County Historical Society, the Salem monthly meetings took place around the old oak tree for more than 300 years. Numerous Friends had been buried in unmarked graves here since 1681 when the 16-acre tract was turned over from Samuel Nicholson and his wife, Ann, for the sum of 12 pounds. The indenture included the old oak tree and the Friends Burial Ground.

If you look carefully, you may be able to spot a slight rise in the ground to the east of the tree where the foundation of a brick house—believed to be the first brick meeting house in the Colonies—had been built around 1700. The graveyard, according to legend, was also the site of an ancient Indian burying ground and a few Indian remains were found at the northern end when buildings were erected.

NOTE: Allow enough time to explore Salem, especially the historic district along Market Street and along Broadway. Many buildings have identifying plaques. The Salem Friends Meetinghouse, built in 1772 in a Flemish-bond pattern of brick (on East Broadway and Walnut) has been in continuous service longer than any religious building in the state.

83

Wheaton Village Garden

LOCATION ❧ Cumberland County
Glasstown Road (off Route 55)
Millville 08332
609-825-6800 or 1-800-998-4552
Web site: www.wheatonvillage.org

GARDEN SIZE ❧ *Village Garden:* Less than ¼ acre. *Grounds:* 88 acres.

ADMISSION ❧ Fee; no charge for children 5 and under

WHEN TO VISIT ❧ April through December, daily 10–5; January
through March closed Mondays and Tuesdays.;
Also closed Easter, Thanksgiving, Christmas, and
New Year's Day.

HIGHLIGHTS ❧ Lovely display of herbs, each marked with a
beautiful tag, and an unusual center fountain.
Nearby Wheaton Glass Factory; stained-glass
studio; folklife center; quaint village shops.

FACILITIES ❧ Rest rooms; water; handicapped-accessible; gift
shop, snack bar, adjacent PaperWaiter Restaurant
& Pub and Country Inn

EVENTS ❧ Among the year-round events is a midwinter glass
weekend, antiques and collectibles show,
paperweight collectors weekend, craft fair, and a
Christmas exhibition. Call for a calendar of
events.

Although thousands of people visit Wheaton Village each year, few
have explored the charming garden located in the Museum of American
Glass courtyard. The garden, begun in 1973 when the museum opened
to the public, may only measure 60 feet by 101 feet, but it's a delightful
place to visit. A brick path beneath a canopy of oaks leads to hidden
nooks where sculptures can be found.

A "rescued" sculpture stands in the Wheaton Village garden in the courtyard of the Museum of American Glass.

According to director Janet Peterson, the Creative Glass Center of America established a fellowship in 1983 for contemporary artists. Those fortunate enough to receive fellowships are allowed to use the glass factory, provided they donate one glass sculpture to the program for exhibit. Since many of the works created are too large to be accommodated inside the museum, they've been placed in what has now become a glass sculpture garden.

A metal fountain— a sculpture of a boy and girl under an umbrella entitled *Out in the Rain*—stands near the center of the garden. According to Dianne Wood, curatorial assistant, this fountain and its base had been displayed at Giuffra's Candy Store in downtown Millville for many years. When the candy store closed, the two parts of the fountain were separated. The figures ended up in Vineland, and the base in Ocean City. Eventually, both were purchased by Mr. Wheaton, who brought them back for all to enjoy.

After touring the garden, don't miss the Museum of American Glass, where over 6,500 glass objects are housed in an elegant blue-and-white Victorian building with gingerbread trim. The museum's four bright, spacious wings surround the open courtyard garden. All styles of glass are represented and include everything from soda bottles, mason jars, and traditional South Jersey designs to exquisite Tiffany and experimental pieces. Also be sure to tour the T.C. Wheaton Glass Factory, visit the General Store, and take a ride on the miniature railroad.

NOTE: Wheaton Village is close to Bridgeton, the state's largest historic district. You might want to stay at the County Inn overnight and spend the next day admiring Bridgeton's unusual architecture, visit a 17th-century Swedish farmstead with a collection of authentically furnished buildings, take the family to the Cohanzick Zoo, or visit the Millville Army Air Field Museum, which recaptures the days when Millville played a primary role in our nation's defense during World War II.

84
Marlpit Hall Garden

LOCATION ❧ Monmouth County
137 King's Highway
Middletown 07748
732-462-1466

GARDEN SIZE ❧ Pocket-sized

ADMISSION ❧ *Garden:* No charge. *House:* Fee.

WHEN TO VISIT ❧ *Garden:* Dawn to dusk daily, year-round. May is
peak bloom for lilacs; June for irises and roses.
House: May 1 through September 30, Tuesday and
Sunday 1–4; Saturday 10–4. The house, closed
for renovations at this writing, is scheduled to
reopen in 1999. Call before visiting.

HIGHLIGHTS ❧ Old lilac, dogwood, boxwood plantings, and old-
fashioned pink roses; sundial; historic house.

FACILITIES ❧ Rest room when the house is open

This tiny garden measures a mere 10 feet by 18 feet. It is a perfect
example of gardens that were planted adjacent to homes in the 1600s;
and it's also a charming place to observe butterflies and bees. Planted
and maintained by the Village Garden Club of Middletown in 1967, the
rectangular garden is surrounded by mature boxwood, lilac, and dogwood. Crushed oyster shells were used for the path leading to the herb
patch, as this was the mulch of choice during Colonial times.

During the summer months, bee balm, lavender, mint, foxglove,
rose tarragon, fennel, and daylilies put on a marvelous show. The lilacs
are at their peak in May, and the irises and fragrant old-fashioned pink
roses are outstanding in June. A beautiful patch of thyme surrounds the
attractive sundial, inscribed: GROW OLD ALONG WITH ME; THE BEST IS YET TO BE.

If Marlpit Hall is open, check out the inside of this interesting
house, also referred to as the Grover-Taylor House. Built as a one-and-

a-half story house in 1686 by James Grover Jr., it was added to by John Taylor between 1740 and 1752. According to the Monmouth County Historical Association, members of the Grover and Taylor families were among the area's leading politicians, farmers, and merchants, and this structure reflects the various lifestyles and tastes of its occupants as well as the early history of Middletown—one of New Jersey's oldest communities and an important village in Colonial times. Owned by the Taylor family until 1936, the property was purchased by the Monmouth County Historical Association and is operated as a museum to capture the history of the town and the Colonial way of life.

85

Leaming's Run Gardens and Colonial Farm

LOCATION ❧ Cape May County
1845 Route 9 North
Cape May Court House 08210
609-465-5871

GARDEN SIZE ❧ 20 acres

ADMISSION ❧ Fee

WHEN TO VISIT ❧ *Gardens:* May 15 through October 20, daily
9:30–5. *Cooperage:* May 15 through Christmas,
daily 10–5. The Cooperage may be visited
independently of the gardens at the Route 9
entrance.

HIGHLIGHTS ❧ Twenty-seven individual gardens on 20 acres; the
largest annual garden in the country;
reconstructed whaler's cabin

FACILITIES ❧ Rest room, water, gift shop; handicapped-
accessible

EVENTS ❧ Guided tours offered June through October.
Hibiscus Week in July; arrival of the
hummingbirds in August; picnicking in October.
Write or call for schedule.

One visit is all it takes to understand why Leaming's Run Gardens and Colonial Farm is considered one of the most beautiful gardens in the country.

When he purchased the white stucco house over 30 years ago, Jack Aprill knew that it had been built and named Leaming Run in 1730 by Christopher Leaming. However, it wasn't until much later that Aprill discovered it was not only one of the oldest houses in Cape May

County, but the only whaler's home still in existence in the state.

Follow the meandering garden paths to enjoy the plantings along a gently flowing stream, in dense woods, and on the banks of a pond. The tea-colored Leaming's Run Brook traverses the property; it can be viewed from different points as a sylvan pond, a moss-banked woodland stream, and a curving river. Rustic bridges over lowland marsh lead to water-loving plants such as cardinal flowers and cattails. Swamp azaleas, sweet pepper bushes, and magnolias provide a delightful natural backdrop for annuals that bloom from May through October.

Each one of the 27 gardens has a theme. The Yellow Garden includes gladiolus, banana pepper, and yellow squash. The yellow gourd vines draping the rustic fence stand in vivid contrast to the lush green lawn; in autumn, this area is aflame with the brilliant foliage of huckleberries and sumac.

The Evening Garden is best seen during morning or evening light, but its colors change throughout the day. In the early hours, morning glories cast a bright blue hue over the garden, but as the sun disappears, they fade into the shadows and white and light-foliated plants, such as dusty miller, beam. During September and October, the chrysanthemums and asters bloom profusely.

Take a moment to linger at the Reflecting Garden, for here dozens of water lilies are mirrored in a pond that's home to bluegills, crappies, perch, minnows, and catfish. The Red and Blue Garden features a colorful kaleidoscope of brilliant flowers, including royal blue lobelia and plum-red celosia.

The Colonial Farm section looks much the same as it did when Leaming settled here in the 1600s. Using logs cut on the property, Aprill reconstructed Leaming's log cabin following old records. Walk inside— you may have to step over a rooster or clucking hen—for a closer look at the fireplace and chimney built of commonly used brick, mud, and twigs. The Cottage Garden is planted with common 18th-century herbs such as thyme, savory, and lovage.

The main garden path eventually leads to a red barn built by Leaming in 1730 as a workshop for building the barrels used to ship whale oil. Now converted to a gift shop called The Cooperage, it holds an amazing array of garden-related gift items.

NOTE: October is the only month picnicking is allowed on the property, but you can bring lunch any time and enjoy it at nearby Cape May County Park (609-465-5271) on US 9. Take a bicycle along so you can explore the park, visit the children's zoo, and check out the summer concerts.

86
The Wetlands Institute Gardens

LOCATION ❧ Cape May County
1075 Stone Harbor Boulevard
Stone Harbor 08247
609-368-1211

GARDEN SIZE ❧ Less than ½ acre

ADMISSION ❧ *Garden:* No charge. *Institute:* Fee.

WHEN TO VISIT ❧ *Garden:* Dawn to dusk daily, year-round. *Institute:* Daily 9:30–4:30; closed Sunday and Monday October 15 through May 15.

HIGHLIGHTS ❧ Beach-hardy plants; exhibit and lecture hall, touch museum, salt water aquarium, library, elevated marsh boardwalk and trail, observation tower, 6,000-acre salt marsh.

FACILITIES ❧ Rest room and water when building is open

EVENTS ❧ Annual Wings'n Water Festival weekend; outdoor classes; guided marsh walks; family-fun days. Call for a schedule.

When Marion Glaspey took on the task of beautifying the grounds of The Wetlands Institute, only a few hollies, bayberries, beach plums, red cedars, and seaside goldenrods adorned the property. These were initially moved here from Herbert Mills' farm in Cumberland County when he founded the institute. Although the soil consisted solely of sand and gravel fill, and the area was subjected to constant wind and salt spray, Glaspey was determined to show visitors that it was possible to grow beautiful flowers in such a hostile environment. To do so, she used her own funds to purchase seeds from catalogs, plants from local nurseries, and brought cuttings from her home garden.

Among the plants Glaspey chose that would thrive at the seashore are trumpet vine, daylilies, and showy coreopsis: The lemon-yellow flowers of this pest-free native American wildflower bloom throughout the summer. Wild and hybrid mallows, butterfly weed, buddleia, cosmos, sunflowers, and hydrangeas bloom in August, and during September and October, the asters are outstanding, attracting not only hundreds of monarch butterflies, but visitors who return year after year.

Glaspey added a great number of ornamental grasses and native shrubs, including the white-flowered shadbush, one of the earliest shrubs to bloom, and the hollies, considered the backbone of the garden. Perennials include hollyhock, joe-pye weed, hardy ageratum, Siberian and bearded irises, liriope, liatris, cardinal lobelia, 'Sir Thomas Lipton' roses, 'Autumn Joy' sedum, yucca, and much more.

If time allows, stroll along the easy, short Salt Marsh Trail, where plants and animals survive the harsh environment in extremes of temperature and salinity, as well as flooding and drying. The vegetation of the salt marsh is diverse; over many years, reed grass, marsh elder, bayberry, groundsel, and other transitional plants have colonized the slightly elevated area, a dredge spill site. Hundreds of small holes in the sand are the burrows of fiddler crabs. Willets, red-wings, and a number of other birds frequent the area, and you might be lucky enough to spot an osprey on the platform above the marsh.

The Wetlands Institute is "dedicated to research and public education concerning wetlands and coastal ecosystems." On the self-guiding tour inside the handsome cedar shake building, you'll learn how important grass harvesting was during Colonial times and how salt marshes distribute their riches through the food chain. At the adjacent Diller Education Center, explore the marsh ecosystem via hands-on exhibits, quiz boards, and games. The live fishes, turtles, and mollusks in tanks, and the panorama of shorebirds and native raptors on display are representative of what's waiting outside if you haven't yet strolled the trail.

Before leaving, climb the spiral stairs for a bird's-eye view of the marshes and surrounding communities, or settle down in the comfortable Herbert Mills Memorial Library, where there are great science and natural history books plus an excellent view of the marsh.

NOTE: During nesting season in early April, thousands of birds find refuge among the dense foliage and nearby marshland at the Stone Harbor Bird Sanctuary. Ask for directions to this bird-watchers' paradise.

87
Butterfly Garden at Cape May Bird Observatory

LOCATION ❧ Cape May County
Northwood Center
701 East Lake Drive,
Cape May Point 08212
609-884-2736
GARDEN SIZE ❧ Less than ¼ acre
ADMISSION ❧ No charge
WHEN TO VISIT ❧ *Garden:* Dawn to dusk daily, year-round. *Northwood*
Center: 10–5 daily, year-round.
HIGHLIGHTS ❧ Butterflies and hummingbirds galore
FACILITIES ❧ Rest room and water when visitors center is open
EVENTS ❧ Call for schedule of garden talks.

Butterflies and hummingbirds don't need a lot of space, but they're very choosy about what they'll dine on. With this in mind, the Flora for Fauna Nursery created a special garden outside the Cape May Bird Observatory for these magnificent creatures.

The monarch, mourning cloak, black swallowtail, and eastern tiger swallowtail are but a few of the many species that frequent this area. This tiny garden also attracts the ruby-throated hummingbird, often mistaken for a large bumblebee because of the loud humming of its wings. If you wait long enough to watch one land or hover at a flower, such as the bee balm and bleeding-heart that are planted here, you'll observe one of the tiniest and most beautiful birds in the world.

Stop in at the observatory, where you can pick up tips on attracting birds and butterflies to your own garden, as well as interesting nature-related gifts. Ask for a schedule of events; you might be there in time for a bird or butterfly workshop or walk.

88
Pavilion Circle Gardens

LOCATION ❧ Cape May County
Cape May and Pavilion Avenues
Cape May Point 08212
609-884-2269

GARDEN SIZE ❧ Less than 2 acres

ADMISSION ❧ No charge

WHEN TO VISIT ❧ Dawn to dusk daily, year-round

HIGHLIGHTS ❧ Individual garden beds, including two with
plantings to draw butterflies; many tree species

FACILITIES ❧ Benches; handicapped-accessible; volleyball court

EVENTS ❧ Entertainment and special children's games on
Saturday nights. Call for a schedule.

One might say this unique garden is a miracle, for initially these grounds contained nothing but a barren patch of dried-out cactus and years of accumulated debris. "In fact," says Sally Sachs, "it was an eyesore and just a way to get from one side of town to the other. My late husband saw its potential and felt the residents were lucky to have an area that was undeveloped . . . he dreamt of the day this wasted space could be developed into gardens."

Unfortunately, her husband died while working out plans for building a garden on this site, but Sally roused her neighbors to help turn his dream into reality. But it wasn't easy. "Roger Wells, a landscape architect and my husband's former partner, donated $35,000 of architectural landscape plans," she recalls, "and we then began the process of getting those plans approved by the town government and various civic groups." After surmounting one bureaucratic roadblock after another, the approval and the funds finally came through and the group received an initial $25,000 to begin construction.

The garden areas resulting from Sally's efforts are now cared for by eager volunteers who call themselves "bedfellows," because three or four people are assigned to each bed. Those who can't do the hard work on their knees are called "bedwarmers," and are responsible for donating the funds to buy the plants. There are also the "rovers"—mostly summer residents or visitors who don't have a permanent bed to care for; they rove around helping out where needed. "Each person who tends a bed looks upon it as one of their children and they're quite serious about taking care of it properly," says Sally. "People like to sit here now that there are plentiful benches all around the gardens, and it's become a meeting place for residents and visitors. What's happened is that an area that was once barren and uninviting is now very user-friendly."

The annual and perennial beds around the perimeter of the huge circle garden were planted by individuals; they contain daylilies, Asiatic daisies, astilbe, periwinkle, chrysanthemums, impatiens, snapdragons, alyssum, Gloriosa daisy, blue salvia, and butterfly weed. The interior beds, planted under the guidance of landscape architects and nurserymen, were designed to lure butterflies; they feature vitex, moonbeam coreopsis, astilbe, black-eyed Susan, joe-pye weed, white and midnight purple buddleia, 'Anthony Waterer' spirea, and summersweet. An herb bed, planted and maintained by a member of the Pennsylvania Horticultural Society, features purple basil, chives, American germander, fernleaf and Dutch lavender, pineapple mint, Italian parsley, rue, several varieties of sage, scented geraniums, and thyme.

Spring brings a spectacular showing of bulbs, such as spring beauty, 'Violet Pearl' hyacinth, 'Angelique' tulip, a mixture of Emperor tulips, and a pink mix of narcissi. The young trees are growing taller by the season, and autumn sets the red maple, flowering plums and willow oak aglow.

While the garden brings joy to residents and visitors alike, it always reminds Sally of her late husband: "Every time I work on planting or weeding at the circle, I think to myself, he knows I'm working out here and we have a pretty place now. He left a wonderful legacy."

89

Historic Cold Spring Village Gardens

LOCATION ❧	Cape May County
	720 Route 9
	Cape May 08204
	609-898-2300
GARDEN SIZE ❧	Less than ¼ acre
ADMISSION ❧	Fee
WHEN TO VISIT ❧	Memorial Day through Father's Day, weekends 10–4:30; Father's Day through Labor Day weekend, daily 10–4:30; weekends in September 10–4:30.
HIGHLIGHTS ❧	Farm and herb garden; 19th-century living-history museum
FACILITIES ❧	Rest room, refreshments, water
EVENTS ❧	Authentically dressed village craftspeople demonstrate age-old crafts using traditional tools, prepare and cook garden herbs, and tend the farm garden.

Journey back to yesteryear at Historic Cold Spring Village, a recreated 19th-century living history museum located three miles north of Victorian Cape May. Take time to examine the farm and cottage gardens in this village, dedicated to preserving the crafts, trades, lifestyles, and architecture of a small South Jersey rural community from more than 150 years ago.

Cold Spring, named for the fresh spring of sparkling water that bubbled up through the salt marshes, was a thriving town during the early 1800s. People came from miles around for its excellent water supply, and it was also the site of the first tidal grist mill. According to village officials, "Rather than depend upon a mill pond for power, the tidal mills operated on water trapped when a creek or stream was at high tide, thus ensuring a source of daily power." By 1840, Cold Spring was an important stagecoach run and a prosperous community boasting a tavern, 2 churches, 2 stores, and 40 homes. Little remains of the original village, but 20 antique buildings were brought from nearby Cape May and Cumberland County and restored on the 22-acre site to recreate the town as it was then. Today the houses are occupied by costumed craftspeople who demonstrate traditional crafts.

At the Farm Garden, you can watch farmers sow and tend the crops as they did in the 1800s, as well as gather and store the harvest for the winter months ahead. Behind the circa-1702 Spicer-Leaming House, reputed to be the second oldest house in lower Cape May County, the mistress of the house can usually be found discussing life in the 1850s while she prepares dinner on the open-hearth beehive oven. If you're there at the right time, you'll probably get to sample the food as well as see her making quick trips to the gardens for herbs.

Typical of early-American gardens, the cottage garden plantings are conveniently located adjacent to the kitchen, and the mistress was responsible for planting and tending the garden. No doubt she loved this particular job, for it was an opportunity to be alone outdoors and admire the beauty of colorful flowers, including petunias and marigolds. Cottage gardens were purposely kept small because there was only so much time in the day to tend them, and they were usually enclosed by a fence, as here, to protect the plants from being crushed by stray livestock or deer. Daylilies, daisies, and old roses adorn this garden; common perennials of the 1800s included columbine, phlox, stonecrop, and garden heliotrope, while biennials included sweet william and hollyhock. Since few spices were available in those days, tasty blossoms—including marigold petals for custard, rose petals to garnish a party cake, and violets for salads—were often used.

90
Hereford Inlet Lighthouse Gardens

LOCATION ❧ Cape May County
First and Central Avenues
North Wildwood 08260
609-522-2955

GARDEN SIZE ❧ More than ½ acre

ADMISSION ❧ No charge; donations accepted

WHEN TO VISIT ❧ *Garden:* Dawn to dusk daily, year-round; the garden is lighted at night. *Lighthouse:* Summer, 9:00–4:45 daily; hours vary the rest of the year.

HIGHLIGHTS ❧ Herb, scent, and ornamental gardens; bird-watching; boardwalk leading to sensational views; unusual historic lighthouse

FACILITIES ❧ Rest room; benches; gazebo for weddings

EVENTS ❧ Craft shows, concerts, and flea market held in summer. Call for a schedule.

During the 19th century, Hereford Inlet Lighthouse was a beacon of safety and assurance to sailors. Today, the gardens surrounding it are a source of peace and pleasure to visitors. Come to explore the lighthouse, admire the garden, listen to the birds, attend a summer concert, or simply stroll the grounds and inhale the fresh salt air at the water's edge, only 100 feet away.

The exceptionally beautiful grounds, which received the Cape May County Chamber of Commerce beautification award in 1991 and 1993, are maintained by North Wildwood's Superintendent of Parks, Steve Murray. Miraculously, since 1986, Murray has created an exquisite cottage-style garden from grounds that were previously just sandy lots. Although the garden appears rustic and unplanned, Murray notes that

The Hereford Inlet Lighthouse Gardens feature salt-tolerant plants.

he succeeded in attaining this effect only after a great deal of prior thought and hard work. To accommodate the harsh conditions—the garden is constantly assaulted by salt sprays and ocean winds and the ground consists of a layer of thin soil on top of sand—Murray chose salt-tolerant native and nonnative plants.

The pretty gazebo, located in the courtyard behind the parking area, is surrounded by roses, and is used for weddings and concerts.

The rear lawn and garden areas attract a tremendous variety of birds, butterflies, and hummingbirds. The plantings, well-suited for the harsh conditions, include over 35 perennial flower varieties. They include bellflower, bearing blue or white flowers in early summer; hollyhock, a colorful summer and early-fall bloomer; thrift, producing pink flowers in late spring; and the obedient plant, a member of the mint family that has pink and white flowers in late summer. Annual plantings vary from year to year, but often include cleome, cosmos, geranium, heliotrope, nicotiana, flossflower, snapdragon, celosia, and aster.

Trees include London plane tree, pear, cherry, Chinese elm, and honey locust. You'll also see Japanese black pine, Eastern red cedar, 'Nellie Stevens' holly, and yucca. The ground covers and vines, including seashore juniper, Japanese honeysuckle, trumpet creeper and Virginia creeper, as well as the ornamental grasses—miscanthus, American beach, spartina, and feather-reed—are all well suited to the harsh environment.

The numerous birdbaths and flowers draw dozens of species not only to the garden area, but to the nearby seawall reachable via a boardwalk. On the way to the water, you'll pass through a wild area filled with beach grasses, native shrubbery, and flower borders. Brown pelicans can be spotted from June through August; the double-crested cormorant appears May through September; brants and bufflehead come November through April; the great black-backed gull, herring gull, and American oystercatcher hang out year-round, and osprey appear from April through September.

Lighthouse buffs are usually surprised to find that, unlike the traditional cylindrical lighthouses found throughout the United States, the Hereford Inlet Lighthouse, listed on the National Register of Historic Places in 1977, is merely a light situated atop a Victorian house. In 1918, the Coast Guard installed an automatic light on a tower outside the building. The house was then closed and remained vacant until 1982, when local residents succeeded in having the state's Department of Environmental Protection take over the building, which was then leased to the City of North Wildwood. Thanks to volunteers, the building was put back into shape. Although the light is now maintained by the U.S. Coast Guard, the former lighthouse keeper's home and garden— funded by donations and the Lighthouse Commission of the City of North Wildwood— are open for visitors to enjoy day and night.

Additional
Gardens

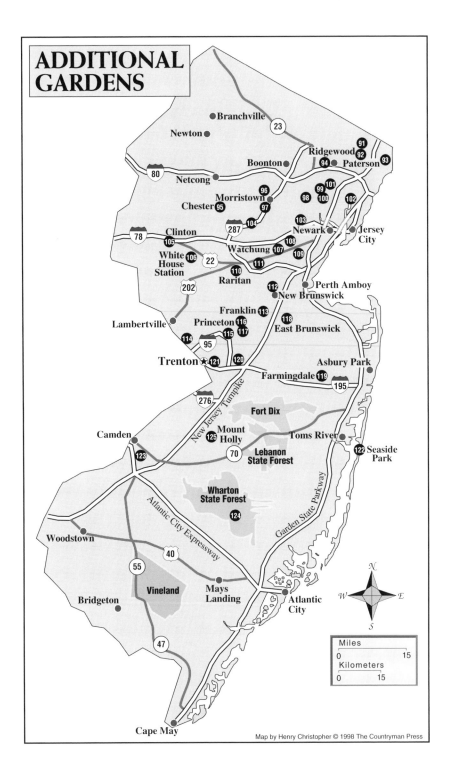

ADDITIONAL GARDENS

Branchville
Newton
23
Ridgewood
91
92
Boonton
94
Paterson
93
Netcong
80
96
99 101
98 100 102
Morristown
Chester 95
97
104
103
Newark
Jersey City
Clinton
287
78 105
108
Watchung 107
White House Station 106
22
109
110 111
202
Raritan
112
Perth Amboy
New Brunswick
Franklin 113
Lambertville
Princeton 116
118
114
115 117
East Brunswick
95
120
Trenton 121
Farmingdale 119
Asbury Park
195
Fort Dix
276
Mount Holly 125
Toms River
Camden
70
Lebanon State Forest
122 Seaside Park
123
Wharton State Forest
124
Garden State Parkway
New Jersey Turnpike
Woodstown
Atlantic City Expressway
40
55
Bridgeton
Vineland
Mays Landing
Atlantic City
47
Cape May

Miles
0   15
Kilometers
0   15

Map by Henry Christopher © 1998 The Countryman Press

Thirty-five Additional, Not-to-be-Missed Gardens, Parks, and Arboretums

91. The Hermitage Gardens

Bergen County; 335 N. Franklin Turnpike, Ho-Ho-Kus 07423; 201-445-8311. Call for hours, no charge.

The Hermitage, situated on 4.9 acres filled with century-old trees and numerous shrubs, is the only 18th–19th-century house in Bergen County designated as a national landmark. Dr. Elijah Rosencrantz, one of Bergen County's earliest physicians, purchased it in 1807, and his descendants lived here for 160 years until the death of its last owner, Mary Elizabeth Rosencrantz. Rather than see developers destroy the house, she bequeathed it to the State of New Jersey in 1970. For more about its interesting history, and a look at the fine collections inside that reflect the property as it appeared in the latter half of the 19th century, arrange for a tour. Also impressive is the authentic replanting of the Victorian landscape as seen in the small garden area outside the bay window, accomplished through dozens of photos Rosencrantz kept. The plantings around the 3-acre property include evergreens and woody material, including boxwoods, lilacs, ferns, geraniums, catnip, Japanese anemones, Siberian irises, and hostas, as well as an herb garden toward the back of the house. There is also a small rose garden with approximately 25 plants. To the left, at the smaller house that's now used as the Hermitage's headquarters, a small garden is maintained by the Wycoff Garden Club with irises, peonies, forget-me-nots, and a descendent of a rose bush brought here from Holland in 1742. There are several benches throughout the property.

92. *James Rose House Garden*

Bergen County; 506 East Ridgewood Avenue, Ridgewood 07450;
201-444-2559. Open by appointment; fee; handicapped-
accessible.

This small house and garden, dating back to 1953, was designed by
James Rose (1913–1991), a recognized genius in landscape architecture
during the 1930s. There is a strong fusion between the house and
garden, since Rose believed in integrated design. Feeling that flowers
took attention away from the main scheme, he designed the garden
with rhododendron, hemlock, Japanese weeping taxus, and a Pagoda
tree surrounding four pool fountains and a scrap metal sculpture spread
upon a bluestone patio that continues into the house. Equally unusual,
the modern house is built of wood, bamboo, glass, fiberglass, and
cinder block that wrap around broad vertical chimneys.

93. *Greenbrook Sanctuary*

Bergen County; Route 9W, Tenafly 07670; 201-768-1360. Open
dawn to dusk daily, year-round; fee for membership.

Although this not-to-be-missed 163-acre nature preserve is for members only, visitors are welcome to call and arrange a time to view the
grounds before applying. It's impossible to describe the sanctuary
beyond saying it's extraordinary, because there is so much to see and do
here. Largely an oak forest, with hickory, black birch, red maple, sweet
gum, elm, pin oak, ash, tupelo, hornbeam, and willow, there are also
common shrubs such as maple-leaf viburnum, witch hazel, laurel,
blueberry, wild azalea, grape, and spicebush. Spring is a great time to
visit; that's when thousands of wildflowers dot the forest floor; the
fiddleheads of 20 species of native ferns unfurl; and dozens of birds are
building their nests. Mushrooms, shelf fungi, and slime molds are
present in late summer and fall, and there's also a sphagnum bog, a
5-acre pond, a 250-foot waterfall, high cliffs, and magnificent views of
the Palisades and Highlands. There's lots of wildlife, too, including red
fox, striped skunk, red and gray squirrels, muskrat, cottontail rabbit,
white-footed mouse, deer, opossum, and weasel. Since 1946, the
Palisades Nature Association has maintained this excellent site.

94. *William Paterson College Outdoor Sculpture Garden*

Passaic County; 300 Pompton Road off Hamburg Turnpike, Wayne 07470; 973-595-2000. Open dawn to dusk daily, year-round; no charge; handicapped-accessible.

On this lush, green, densely wooded 250-acre campus exists a virtually unknown garden paradise—complete with 17 magnificent sculptures—all surrounded by heather, laurel, pine, and juniper. In spring, a carpet of brightly colored wildflowers creates a dazzling scene. One of the most unusual works on the grounds is *Reversal*, a 10-foot-high sculpture created by Elaine Lorenz. It envelops a living juniper bush and is regularly irrigated with hoses buried in shelves of the split concrete cones. Don't miss the small garden in front of Hobart Mansion—the former estate of Garret Hobart, vice president during the McKinley administration—or Ben Shahn Hall and Galleries, where students' works are displayed.

95. *Devereux Deerhaven Gardens*

Morris County; 230 Pottersville Road, Chester 07930; 908-879-4500. Open one day a year; fee.

Although this garden is only open to the public one day a year, it's well worth seeing. Here, at the Devereux Deerhaven School, emotionally disturbed girls and young women nurture plants both on the grounds and in the greenhouse. Voted the Best Healing Garden by *Garden Design* magazine in 1995, and cited by the National Gardening Association, the gardens were originally created for Elizabeth and Alfred Kay in the 1920s. Following their original landscape design, the gardens were replanted by students enrolled in the school's horticultural therapy program. Surrounded by fieldstone walls, fountains, pools, streams, a pergola, and a moongate, plantings include roses, peonies, foxgloves, irises, lupines, snapdragons, and a variety of herbs. Yellow flag and Siberian irises are found along the streambanks, and there is also a profusion of oriental poppies, peonies, and pinks.

96. *Fosterfields Vegetable Garden*

Morris County; 73 Kahdena Road, Morristown, off Route 510; 973-326-7645. Open April 1 through October 29, Wednesday through Saturday 10–5, and NOON–5 on Sunday; fee.

The Fosterfields Vegetable Garden is part of a living-history farm.

On this living-history farm, complete with cows, work horses, chickens, pigs, and sheep, visitors are invited to help with the milking, watering and feeding of animals, and ongoing chores—including planting, weeding, and harvesting peppers, tomatoes, red cabbages, and more, in a turn-of-the-century vegetable garden. The large spruce trees near the garden date back over a century, and the handsome orchard has Black Tartarian and sour cherries; Seckle, Kiefer, and Bartlett Pears; Baldwin, Rhode Island Greening, Northern Spy, and McIntosh apples.

97. *Cross Estate Gardens*

Morris County; in Morristown National Historical Park, Jockey Hollow Area, on Old Jockey Hollow Road off Tempe Wick Road, Morristown 07960; 973-539-2085. Open dawn to dusk daily, year-round; no charge; handicapped-accessible.

This fine example of an English country garden was preserved largely thanks to Jean Pope, a former Chester resident, who began a volunteer project to bring the nearly obscured gardens back to their original condition in 1977. Wide paths crisscross the garden, begun by Royal Horticultural Society member Julia Cross in 1929 with the help of noted

The Cross Estate Gardens are in the English country garden style.

landscape architect Clarence Fowler. Today the restored gardens consist of a formal walled garden, a vine-covered pergola, a mountain laurel allée, an area for sun- and shade-loving native plants, shade gardens planted with ferns, shrubs and perennials; and an overlook with azaleas and naturalized daffodils. Mature lilacs and specimen trees and shrubs include dawn redwood, Franklin tree, Kousa cherry, Florida dogwood, English and American hollies, star magnolia, and a Kentucky coffee tree. Daylilies and daffodils are profuse in spring, followed by dahlias, hostas, periwinkles, and more. The estate, dating back to 1905, includes an impressive mansion, a five-story stone water tower, a gate house and a carriage house. Three years after Mrs. Cross died, her estate was given to the Morristown National Historical Park. Today, the gardens are maintained by volunteers who meet here on Wednesday mornings from April through December, the New Jersey Historical Garden Foundation, and the National Park Service.

98. *Glenmont Gardens*

Essex County; at Edison National Historic Site, Main Street and Lakeside, Llewellyn Park, West Orange 07052; 973-736-0550. Open year-round; hours vary; fee; partially handicapped-accessible.

Thomas Edison and his second wife, Mina Miller, loved adding to the plantings on these 13 acres they purchased in 1886. Until his death in 1931, they had a full-time staff to help them tend the flower gardens, exotic trees and shrubs, and lawn areas. Here you'll also find fragrant lilacs, ferns, and many fruit trees tended by the National Park Service. A bonus is a tour of Edison's laboratory, now a national museum.

99. *Van Vleck Arboretum*

> Essex County; on the grounds of the Montclair Art Museum, 5 South Mountain Avenue, Montclair 07042; 973-746-5555. Open dawn to dusk daily, year-round; no charge.

The plantings on this 3.5-acre spot—a great place to get a close-up view of nature and outdoor sculpture—began in the 1940s when Howard Van Vleck, trustee, architect, artist, and horticulturist, planted an Atlas cedar at the front entrance of the Montclair Art Museum, and rare shrubs from his own garden on the rest of the grounds. Plantings include rhododendron hybrids, a variety of azaleas, dozens of trees— such as the Fringe, Cornelian cherry, maidenhair, Macedonian pine, umbrella pine, willow oak, Scholar, Japanese yew, Canadian hemlock, and leatherleaf viburnum, along with countless shrubs, including the Gold Dust aucuba, wintergreen barberry, Peegee hydrangea, English holly, Chinese juniper, and andromeda. A map locating the major plantings is located near the main entrance. After enjoying the outside grounds, check out the art collection inside.

100. *Walther House Garden*

> Essex County; 474 Upper Mountain Avenue, Montclair 07042; 973-783-5974. Open dawn to dusk daily; no charge.

A joy to behold, this pocket-sized Victorian Garden is especially lovely during spring and summer, when the hostas, boxwoods, rhododendrons, bluebells, buttercups, and a rock garden filled with sedum are all in bloom. Adjacent to the garden is the circa-1845 Walther House, listed on the National Register of Historic Homes. It now serves as headquarters for the Citizens' Committee of the Presby Memorial Iris Garden.

The Walther House Garden is especially appealing in spring and summer.

101. Oakeside Bloomfield Cultural Center Gardens

Essex County; 240 Belleville Avenue, Bloomfield 07003; 973-429-0960. Call for hours; no charge for garden; fee for house tour.

Japanese maple, pin oak, and an ancient magnolia adorn this historic 3.5-acre property where the former rose, kitchen, ornamental, vegetable, and water gardens are being restored to their former splendor. Don't miss the unusual solarium garden inside this 1895 house that was built by the Oakes family, operators of a woolen mill in Bloomfield from 1830 to 1945.

102. Richard W. DeKorte Park

Bergen County; 2 DeKorte Park Plaza, Lyndhurst 07071; 201-460-8300. Open dawn to dusk daily, year-round; no charge; partially handicapped-accessible.

This park and its plantings are a miracle come true, for this 110-acre oasis, situated within 6 miles from New York City and within droning distance of the New Jersey Turnpike, was created from landfill. The best way to see the plantings is by foot along the short, easy, marked trails. Pick up a map inside the Environmental Center where, after the walk, you can visit the unique Trash Museum. The Kingsland Overlook Trail, an experimental 6-acre side slope of a landfill with native plant communities, includes a wildflower and butterfly meadow, grassland meadow, and deciduous and evergreen forest. The Marsh Discovery Trail, a ½-mile boardwalk connecting a series of dredge spill islands, features nature observation blinds, traverses the only known nesting site of the ruddy duck in New Jersey, and supports many marsh plants. To see over 52 species of woody and herbaceous plants, try the Lyndhurst Nature Reserve Trail, with outstanding bayberry, dogwood, and chokeberry.

103. Taylor Park

Union County; Millburn Avenue and Main Street, Millburn 07041; 973-564-7058. Open dawn to dusk daily; no charge; handicapped accessible.

Formerly a pasture, these grounds were presented to the Township of Millburn in 1924 by Mrs. John Taylor. The cows are gone, but in their place is a well-planned park with mountain laurels, rhododendrons, giant sycamores, and a variety of shrubs. The cherry trees, donated in 1966, are a memorial to the Vietnam veterans. A natural stream flows through the park, where there are tennis courts, rest rooms, and a huge lawn to stretch out on, but my favorite spot within this park is the Wallbridge Rose Garden. Created in 1981 by the Short Hills Garden Club and dedicated in memory of Mr. and Mrs. William Wallbridge, it consists of a huge gazebo surrounded by hundreds of roses arranged in attractive beds easily reachable by wide walkways. The trees in this area, consisting of oak, cherry, sycamore, and spruce, are also striking.

104. Lord Stirling Park Gardens

Somerset County; 190 Lord Stirling Road, Basking Ridge 07920; 908-766-2489. Open 9–5 daily; no charge; partially handicapped-accessible.

These are gardens in progress, but well worth seeing at any time. There are three main garden areas close to an attractive pond in back of the center, namely the Native Plant Wildlife Demonstration Garden, the Composting Garden, and the Track Garden. Many of the beds, used for education programs scheduled throughout the year, include native New Jersey annuals and perennials. All plants are labeled. There are numerous evergreens and vines, and a butterfly zone at one end of the building filled with larvae and nectar sources. Don't miss hiking one of the many trails through 430 acres of marsh, swamp, field, and forest for a look at a wide variety of flowering plants. Skunk cabbage emerges as early as February; trout lilies and spring beauties burst open by April; summer awakens the water hemlock, Indian hemp, swamp rose mallow, English plantain, pokeweed, and more; while autumn is aglow with goldenrods and asters.

105. Clinton Historical Museum Gardens

Hunterdon County; 56 Main Street off Route 78, Clinton 08809. Open April 1 through October 31, 10–4 daily; fee; handicapped-accessible.

Beside the historic circa-1810 mill overlooking the picturesque south branch of the Raritan River, is a lovely pocket-sized garden in memory of Elena Vaida. Called A Mother's Garden, and donated by Tony and Cynthia Vaida and friends in 1984, it is maintained by the Hunterdon Hills Garden Club, and arranged with a Peace rose in the center circle with various beds around it. These contain azaleas, chrysanthemums, daylilies, coralbells, plantain lilies, climbing roses, Oriental poppies, grasses, cornflowers, stonecrop, spirea, and mother-of-thyme. The thoughtfully placed bench is perfect for resting and admiring the beautiful plants. There is also an attractive herb garden in back of the log cabin further up the road; it's filled with plantings typical of those grown in Colonial times. As a bonus, explore the village with its blacksmith shop, turn-of-the-century general store and post office, 1860 schoolhouse, and agricultural and commercial artifacts.

106. The Ryland Inn Gardens

Hunterdon County; Route 22 West, Whitehouse 08888; 908-634-4011. Open dawn to dusk daily, year-round; no charge; handicapped-accessible.

Located on 50 acres, the Ryland Inn shines not only for its highly acclaimed restaurant but also for its picturesque, gently rolling setting amid a grove of magnificent beeches and oaks. Many weddings and parties are held here for the romantic outdoor setting, complete with a Victorian gazebo, garden bridal cottage, and profuse flowering gardens. There's also an impressive 8-acre herb garden with over 150 herbs, including pimpernel and rosemary, and more than 120 varieties of vegetables planted in the vegetable garden that Chef Craig Shelton uses in preparing his gourmet delights. Even if you don't eat here (and you should, because the fine meals and elegant country atmosphere are unforgettable), do plan on strolling the beautifully manicured grounds.

107. *Watchung Reservation Gardens*

> Union County; Coles Avenue and New Providence Road (north of Route 22), Mountainside 07092; 908-789-3670. Open dawn to dusk daily; no charge; handicapped-accessible.

Thanks to the Rake and Hoe Garden Club, visitors to the Butterfly Garden can admire a great variety of winged creatures, including the black and anise swallowtails, monarch, mourning cloak; great spangled fritillary, and little cabbage—since they flock to the special plantings placed here just for them in the 1980s. Plantings include phlox, buddleia, zinnia, cosmos, sage, milkweed, and others. There is also a Backyard Habitat Garden, planted by the Eagle Scouts, to demonstrate what can be done in a home garden to attract wildlife as an alternative to mowing lawns; and the W. Richmond Tracy Memorial Herb Garden, filled with lemon balm, chives, thyme, garlic, peppermint, tarragon, parsley, and basil. All are located near the Watchung Reservation Visitor Center where, as a bonus, you can watch a planetarium show, examine displays, and pick up a map of the trails within the park.

108. *Stage House Inn Herb Garden*

> Union County; 366 Park Avenue, Scotch Plains 07076; 908-322-4224. Open dawn to dusk daily; no charge; handicapped-accessible.

Chef David Drake began this pocket-sized garden shortly after purchasing the Stage House Inn. As its proprietor and chef, he first planted mint for use in his desserts and fresh herb mix. Just as his clientele has grown, so has the garden. Today, it's bursting with Japanese cucumbers, chicory, a variety of thyme and basil, baby carrots, radishes, hyssop, French tarragon, and more. Decorated with morning glories, a beautiful Japanese maple in the center of the garden, and attractive azaleas and dahlias, it's the perfect place to sit and enjoy a drink. Or, step inside the 1737 building and treat yourself to lunch or dinner in the charming interior, and taste some of the herbs you admired outside.

109. *Mindowaskin Park*

Union County; 425 East Broad Street, Westfield 07090; 908-233-3148. Open 7 AM-10 PM daily, year-round; no charge; handicapped-accessible.

Named for a Lenni-Lenape Indian chief, this large park, established in 1918, sits in the center of a business district. With its abundant shrubbery, trees, perennials, annual plantings, Victorian lamps, benches, large lake, fountains, playground, gazebo, and winding paths, it's the perfect spot to get away from it all—especially during spring when the trees and flowers bloom. Model boat sailing, art shows, and performances often take place here; call for a schedule.

110. *Duke Island Park*

Somerset County; Off York Road (Route 567), Parking Lot D along the Raritan River, Raritan 08869; 908-722-1200. Open dawn to dusk daily; no charge.

Walking along this part of the Raritan River is a joy, especially in spring, for here you'll find one of the largest wild-bluebell displays in the state. There's also Dutchman's-breeches, a small spreading plant covered with tiny white pantaloon-shaped flowers; the European wood anemone, with white, lavender, or pink starlike flowers; bright yellow leopard's bane, with toothed heart-shaped leaves; and the marsh marigold; but watch out for poison ivy. The level path eventually leads to a dam, a nice spot to have lunch, fish, or listen to the water as it tumbles over rocks. The park also has ballfields, numerous picnic areas, a visitors center, and rest rooms.

111. *Atlock Farm Garden*

Somerset County; 545 Weston Canal Road, Somerset 08873; 732-356-3373. Hours vary seasonally; call for schedule; no charge.

Although this is a commercial nursery business, it is well worth visiting, for horticulturist/owner Ken Selody has created unusual gardens on the premises that demonstrate how plant materials can be adapted for use in home gardens. The impressive Red Border Garden consists of plants and trees that have all tones of red either in the foliage or flowers. At its peak in August, this area features a purple-leaf plum tree, a lovely castor bean plant, a native pokeweed bearing dark purple berries; fuchsias, cannas, and a ruby-laced honey locust tree. In the Coleus Garden, there are more than 100 specimens. Stepping-stones lead into the Herb Garden; a grouping of Scotch thistle attracts dozens of goldfinches. Inside the topiary greenhouse, you'll hear what Ken calls an "eclectic selection of music." Does he feel that music makes the plants grow better? "No," says Ken. "I don't believe that plants have ears. The music is for us. If you believe that plants like music, you'd have to assume that some like classical, others would like jazz or rock-and-roll. So I play what I like."

112. *The Frog and the Peach Barrel Garden*

Middlesex County; 29 Dennis Street at Hiram Square, New Brunswick 08901; 732-846-3216. Open dawn to dusk daily; no charge; handicapped-accessible.

You may be disappointed when you first step out of your car, but the dozens of wooden tubs filled with a variety of herbs, including basil, sage, sorrel, and mint, demonstrate how easy it is to have a lovely little pocket-sized garden just about anywhere. This one is located at a historic circa-1876 renovated industrial building-turned-restaurant, where chef Eric Hambrecht uses the herbs to enrich his dishes. In this

The Frog and the Peach Barrel Garden

unlikely location, the herbs are thriving despite the fact that they're growing next to the parking lot. During the summer months, dozens of baskets filled with colorful annuals hang in and around the restaurant's patio, which is planted with fountain grass, variegated ivy, canna lilies, and many perennials. You'll also see serviceberry, a native tree with edible berries, planted in large pots along a lattice wall; a climbing hydrangea on pillars supporting pots planted with fountain grass; black-eyed Susans; clematis; and a wisteria vine. The lovely plantings, designed and maintained by James Black, a co-owner of the restaurant and a landscape architect, are proof that it's possible to create a garden within a small space in a bustling city. While you're here, take time for lunch or dinner; Hambrecht's modern American cuisine has received rave reviews from numerous publications.

113. *Van Wickle House Garden*

> Somerset County; 1289 Easton Avenue, Franklin Township 08873; 732-828-7418. Hours vary; no charge; partially handicapped-accessible.

Spending a couple of hours here is like a breath of fresh air, for besides the attractive double bench to rest on while taking in the beautiful plantings beneath the shade supplied by the wooden arbor, a brick path leads to a lovely garden filled with larkspur and a host of colorful wildflowers. A short walk over a boardwalk guides visitors to a marshy area where cattails swing to and fro in the slightest breeze; muskrats remove leaves and stems of nearby plants to build their homes; blue flag irises, daylilies, marsh mallows, broad-leafed arrowheads, and yellow pond lilies refresh the spirit, while birds, bees, hummingbirds, and frogs provide the free entertainment.

114. *George Washington Memorial Arboretum*

> Mercer County; Washington Crossing State Park, 355 Washington Crossing Penn Road, Washington Crossing 08691; 609-737-0623. Open dawn to dusk daily; no charge.

This garden is exquisite during spring, when ornamental cherries, crab apples, and dogwoods reach their peak. But it's worth a visit in any season because the huge lawn creates a perfect backdrop for the assortment of trees commonly found throughout the state. A few of those on the grounds include the persimmon, American beech, honey locust, tamarack, sweet gum, tulip poplar, Osage orange, sweet bay magnolia, hop hornbeam, sourwood, Norway spruce, quaking aspen, willow oak, and loblolly pine. Maintained by the Division of Parks and Forestry, the arboretum is close to the Delaware River site that General George Washington crossed on Christmas night in 1776. It is also adjacent to the Johnson Ferry House Garden

115. *Lawrenceville School Arboretum*

> Mercer County; Lawrenceville Road, Lawrence Township 08638; 609-896-0400. Open dawn to dusk daily, year-round; no charge; handicapped-accessible.

Take a delightful self-guiding tour through the heart of the Lawrenceville School campus. Designed by Frederick Law Olmsted in 1886, the grounds contain over 300 species of trees and shrubs. You'll find scarlet oak, pin oak, sugar maple, Canadian hemlock, and a Swiss stone pine, plus red ash, thornless honey locust, northern Catalpa, and butternut hickory. There's also a Kentucky coffee tree, fringe tree, Chinese elm, golden-rain tree, European beech, and the cedar of Lebanon. It's best to bring a tree identification book along since many of them aren't tagged, but you'll know you've reached the thornless Osage orange when you spot its huge baseball-sized fruits on the ground, or the sweet gum when you step on its prickly spherical fruits. Don't worry about getting lost; students are always around to direct you back to the parking area.

116. *Princeton Battlefield State Park*

> Mercer County; 500 Mercer Road/Princeton Pike, Princeton 08540; 609-921-0074. Open year-round Wednesday through Saturday 10–noon and 1–4; Sunday 1–4; no charge; handicapped-accessible.

This is where, on January 3, 1777, Washington defeated the rear guard of the British Army in what is considered to be the fiercest fight for its size during the American Revolution. Dedicated in 1946, this park contains 85 acres of rolling lawn and a hardwood forest consisting of sycamore, beech, and maple; and the Mercer oak—where the Battle of Princeton began—is awesome despite the many cables supporting its huge branches and the concrete reinforcing its trunk. The tree is the symbol of the New Jersey Division of Parks and Forestry, the New Jersey

Green Acres Program, Mercer County, Princeton Township, and many other groups. Besides other specimen trees found on these grounds, the park also features good bird-watching opportunities; the Thomas Clarke House Historic Site, a 1772 farmhouse around which the battle was fought and which housed the dying and the wounded from both armies; an Ionic colonnade, originally part of an 1836 Philadelphia home; and a stone patio marking the grave of British and Americans killed in battle. The vast rolling lawn is perfect for kite flying, ball and Frisbee games, or for viewing the Battle Anniversary (January 3), the July 4 celebration, or the Christmas in 1776 reenactment.

117. *Princeton Institute Woods*

Mercer County; Springdale and Hardin Roads, Princeton 08540; 609-734-8205. Open dawn to dusk daily, year-round; no charge.

There's a great deal of variety in this densely wooded area. Walk the level trail to see masses of pickerel weed in the swampy area, and a huge variety of trees, including the silver maple, box elder, tulip, black gum, birch, dogwood, and hickory. During spring, the forest floor is aglow with thousands of wildflowers, such as jewelweed, pink lady's slipper, dogtooth violet, mayapple, spring beauty, and much more. Bring tree, bird, or wildflower identification books along.

118. *Great Oak Park*

Middlesex County; Winton Road off Rues Lane, East Brunswick 08816; 732-390-6899. Open dawn to dusk daily; no charge; handicapped-accessible.

This 5-acre park features an awesome 250-year-old white oak. Stretching its wide branches outward, it seemingly beckons visitors to come closer to examine its light gray bark patterned with flat, broad ridges and, in autumn, its fiery red foliage. Dedicated in 1996, the park offers picnic grounds, and in the works is a gazebo and an A–Z grouping of trees, each identified alphabetically by the botanical name.

119. *Allaire Village Herb Garden*

Monmouth County; Allaire State Park, Route 524, Exit 98 off the Garden State Parkway, Farmingdale 07727; 732-938-2253 or

The Allaire Village Herb Garden is adjacent to a cottage that was built circa 1827.

732-938-2371. Call for hours; no charge; handicapped-
accessible.

Allaire Village in itself is worth the trip, for in this restored 19th-century
village, guides and craftspersons in period dress demonstrate black-
smithing, carpentry, spinning, weaving, and open-hearth cooking. But
the small herb garden in front of the circa-1827 Foreman's Cottage is

interesting as well. According to Diane Lingsch, the foreman grew herbs in a garden similar to this one for food as well as for medicine. Rosemary and Italian parsley were used in soups and stews; chives added an onionlike flavor to foods; basil was used for vinegar and in egg and tomato dishes; and the fernlike tansy at the front gate is a bitter herb that went well with bacon, meatloaf, and pork. There's also yarrow, used for its spicy flavor when cooked and to clean wounds and improve the complexion; lavender, used for its fragrance, and chamomile, to soothe teething babies and calm nervousness and insomnia.

120. *Bernard Foley Park*

> Mercer County; Nottingham Way and Mercer Street, Hamilton 08690; 609-890-3630. Open dawn to dusk daily; no charge; handicapped-accessible.

Dedicated in 1977 to honor Chief Bernard Foley of the Nottingham Volunteer Fire Department and the men and women of Hamilton Township who lost their lives in the service of their country, this pocket-sized corner garden is a delightful place to sit, watch the birds, listen to the water tumbling from the fountain, and admire an array of annuals, including dusty millers, geraniums, and double baskets of dazzling pansies hanging from old-fashioned lampposts. The Japanese maples provide shade on the hottest summer days.

121. *State Capitol Complex Gardens*

> Mercer County; The State House, West State Street, Trenton 08625; 609-292-4661. Open dawn to dusk daily; no charge; handicapped-accessible.

Unknown to most visitors who journey to the Capitol complex, is a series of garden areas that are nestled between the State House and annex building. Particularly attractive in the spring when the flowering cherry trees, azaleas, and tulips awaken, summer is a good time to visit as well. That's when annual plantings of thousands of zinnias, marigolds, and other beauties can be seen. After, tour the State House, the State Museum (609-292-6347), Trent House Gardens (609-989-3027), and the Old Barracks Museum (609-396-1776).

122. *Karl Ninnemann, Jr. Memorial Butterfly Garden*

Ocean County; Island Beach State Park, Central Avenue, Seaside Park 08752; 732-793-1698. Open dawn to dusk daily; fee; handicapped-accessible.

This pocket-sized butterfly garden, dedicated to a man who shared his love and knowledge of the natural world, is planted with flowers chosen to last throughout the butterfly season. Maintained by naturalist Trish Schuster, Diane Bennett of the New Jersey Shore Audubon Society, and volunteers, it contains columbine, black-eyed Susan, buddleia, wild bergamot, aster, tickseed, and bee balm. Sedum, a late bloomer, attracts the monarch butterfly at the start of its migration in late August until early October. A visit to the nearby Aeolium is a bonus, for inside this tiny exhibit center, you'll not only gain a better understanding of plants that grow in this wind-swept area, but if you walk the short trail starting outside the building, you'll find prickly pear aglow with brilliant yellow flowers in June, a dwarf red cedar forest, bayberry, and shadbush. Be aware of the poison ivy that thrives here.

123. *Helen C. Branson Herb Garden*

Camden County; Greenfield Hall/Historical Society of Haddonfield, 343 Kings Highway East, Haddonfield; 609-429-7375. Call for hours; no charge; handicapped-accessible.

Tucked next to Greenfield Hall—a Classic Revival mansion whose oldest section dates back to 1732 and is now headquarters of the Historical Society of Haddonfield—is a small, attractive herb garden. Planted by the Haddonfield Garden Club in 1976, it features numerous medicinal and culinary herbs similar to those used during Colonial times. Included in the collection are lemon thyme, sage, oregano, sorrel, lamb's ear, lavender, comfrey, chervil, chives, and lungwort. Each grouping is easily identified by attractive markers. A rattan beehive, similar to the skeps used during that era to entice bees to pollinate the herbs, stands in the center of the garden, which is surrounded by ancient boxwood.

124. *Batsto Village Gardens*

Burlington County; in Wharton State Forest off Route 542, Washington Township 07675; 609-561-3262. Open dawn to dusk daily; no charge except for a tour of the mansion and for parking from Memorial through Labor Day; handicapped-accessible.

This small Victorian demonstration garden, filled with herbs similar to those the mansion owners used in the 1800s, is divided into two beds. A variety of herbs, including foxglove, grown for its beauty and healing powers; New Jersey tea, bronze fennel, many varieties of thyme, and scented geraniums are grown inside the formal beds, while antique roses, gourds, and sunflowers adorn the edges. There are also pots filled with peppermint and roses. The garden is at its best during summer. As a bonus, stroll through the 19th-century village, watch the crafts-persons dressed in period attire working at various tasks, and take the short, easy trail through the wooded area.

125. *Smithville Mansion Courtyard Gardens*

Burlington County; Smithville Road, Eastampton 08060; 609-265-5068. Open dawn to dusk daily; no charge; fee for mansion tours offered Wednesday and Sunday.

Beautiful gardens filled with iris, azalea, boxwood, and annuals grace this 1840s Greek Revival mansion on the grounds of a 19th-century manufacturing complex.

New Jersey Garden Organizations

The Garden Club of New Jersey, Inc., Holly House, 126 Ryders Lane, East Brunswick; 732-249-0947. For information on garden clubs throughout the state.

The Garden Conservancy, PO Box 219, Cold Spring, New York 10516; 914-265-2029. Instrumental in preserving noteworthy gardens in the US and in fostering appreciation for gardening throughout the country; Annual Open Day event offers public admission to exceptional private gardens.

Committee for the Advancement of Arboriculture: 908-431-7903

Jersey Shore Rose Society: 732-462-2816

New Jersey Daffodil Society: 973-763-8531

New Jersey Division of Parks and Forestry: 609-984-0370

New Jersey Forest Resource Education Center: 609-984-0620

New Jersey Forestry Association: 609-771-8301

New Jersey Shade Tree Federation: 732-246-3210

New Jersey State Chrysanthemum Society: 973-992-6197

New Jersey State Forest Education Center: 732-928-0029

New Jersey State Forest Services: 609-292-2520

Skylands Association: 973-962-9634

Society of American Foresters (NJ Division): 609-586-6903

Rutgers Cooperative Extension Service: 732-932-9306

Above and Beyond

The New Jersey Flower and Patio Show is held annually in March at the Garden State Exhibit Center, Somerset; 732-785-9174. Excellent exhibitions featuring current gardening trends; professionally landscaped gardens filled with blooming color; lectures; floral arrangements. The 32nd show was held in 1998.

Bibliography

Barash, Cathy Wilkinson. *Edible Flowers from Garden to Palate*. Golden, Colo.: Fulcrum, 1993. Learn how to add flavor and color to your cuisine by using your own garden imaginatively. A combination cookbook and gardening guide, it showcases 280 recipes using flowers from herbs, vegetables, and ornamentals.

———. *Evening Gardens*. Shelburne, Vt.: Chapters, 1993. A guide to creating a garden or adding touches to an existing one that comes to life when the sun goes down.

Burnie, David. *Plant*. New York: Knopf, 1989. Well-illustrated description of everything you want to know about a plant; what it is, how it blooms, how it is pollinated, how the seeds are spread, and what happens if there aren't any seeds.

Choroszewski, Walter. *The Garden State in Bloom*. Somerville, N.J.: Aesthetic Press, 1993. Lovely photos and short descriptions of a few of New Jersey's gardens in a large-format book.

Cork, Barbara. *Mysteries and Marvels of Plant Life*. London: Usborne, 1989. An exciting and detailed look at many of the amazing and mysterious aspects of nature.

Dunning, Joan. *Secrets of the Nest*. New York: Houghton Mifflin, 1994. An original view of the lives of North American birds, their eggs and nests, mating, and behavior.

Ellis, Barbara W. *Burpee Complete Gardener*. New York: Macmillan, 1995. Full of solid information covering garden basics such as pruning, propagation, staking, division, and harvesting. Included are suggestions for a low-maintenance garden, a potted garden, a herb garden, and one grown from seed. Beautifully illustrated.

Johnson, Lady Bird and Carlton B. Lees. *Wildflowers Across America* New York: Abbeville, 1993. A tribute to one of this nation's loveliest natural resources and a strong plea for increasing the use of native plants and wildflowers is contained in this beautifully illustrated book.

Kowalchik, Claire. *Rodale's Illustrated Encyclopedia of Herbs.* Emmaus, Pa.: Rodale, 1987. An endless source of useful information and herbal know-how presented in an A–Z format with easy-to-use charts and lists.

Kraska, Martha E. *Burpee American Gardening Series: Herbs.* New York: Prentice-Hall, 1993. Complete cultural information, plus scores of tips and essential information on both common and uncommon herbs.

Martin, Laura C. *Garden Flower Folklore.* Old Saybrook, Conn.: Globe Pequot, 1987. If you've ever wondered how foxglove got its name or why pansies are considered highly nutritional, you'll find the answers here. Entries are organized according to the season in which the plants bloom, complete with pen-and-ink drawings and a description of the botanical characteristics of each plant.

————. *Wildflower Folklore.* Old Saybrook, Conn.: Globe Pequot, 1984. A collection of biographies of the most interesting and well-known wildflowers in the world. Grouped according to flower color, the book offers physical descriptions, scientific and common names, and information on where and when they grow, along with interesting notes about the unique history and personality of each plant.

Ortiz, Elisabeth. *The Encyclopedia of Herbs, Spices & Flavorings.* New York: Dorling Kindersley, 1994. This volume has 750 full-color photographs, more than 185 recipes, and information on more than 200 herbs, edible flowers, and leaves, plus a history of all these ingredients.

Peattie, Donald Culross. *A Natural History of Trees of Eastern and Central North America.* Boston, Mass.: Houghton Mifflin, 1991. A detailed handbook with clear descriptions, a key to genera and species, and complete historical information about native America's trees.

Pyle, Robert Michael. *Handbook for Butterfly Watchers.* New York: Houghton Mifflin, 1992. Covering everything from ecology to photography to butterfly gardening, this book is fascinating and well illustrated.

Recknagel, Alice. *Burpee American Gardening Series: Garden Designs.* New York: Prentice-Hall, 1993. Forty gardens to fit every taste and budget from an easy, carefree garden to a formal rose garden.

Roach, Margaret. *Burpee American Gardening Series: Groundcovers.* New York: Prentice-Hall, 1993. A marvelous description of groundcovers, vines, and grasses, with special chapters on designing, planting, and growing, plus information on pests and diseases and more.

Roth, Charles E. *The Wildlife Observer's Guidebook.* New York: Prentice-Hall, 1982. A complete manual of tips and techniques for watching and studying wild animals throughout the year no matter where you live.

Stokes, Donald W. *The Natural History of Wild Shrubs and Vines.* Old Saybrook, Conn.: Globe Pequot, 1981. This book makes each of us stop to absorb the beauty of gardens, and describes how plants grow, why they take certain shapes, and how their different parts function.

Wells, Diana. *100 Flowers and How They Got Their Names.* Chapel Hill, N.C.: Algonquin, 1997. Describes the flowers we pick, how we came to know and love them, and tidbits about historic figures and more.

Zatz, Arline. *Best Hikes with Children in New Jersey.* Seattle: The Mountaineers, 1992. Seventy-five hikes from the easy to the difficult, 1–8 miles in length, throughout the state.

————. *New Jersey's Special Places.* Woodstock, Vt.: The Countryman Press, 1994. Recommendations of scenic, historic, and cultural treasures in the Garden State.

Index